Diabetic Air Fryer Cookbook

1800 Days Low Carb, Low Sugar, Delicious and Easy-to-Cook Recipes to Manage Diabetic Diet, Includes 28-Day Meal Plan

Janelle M. Neel

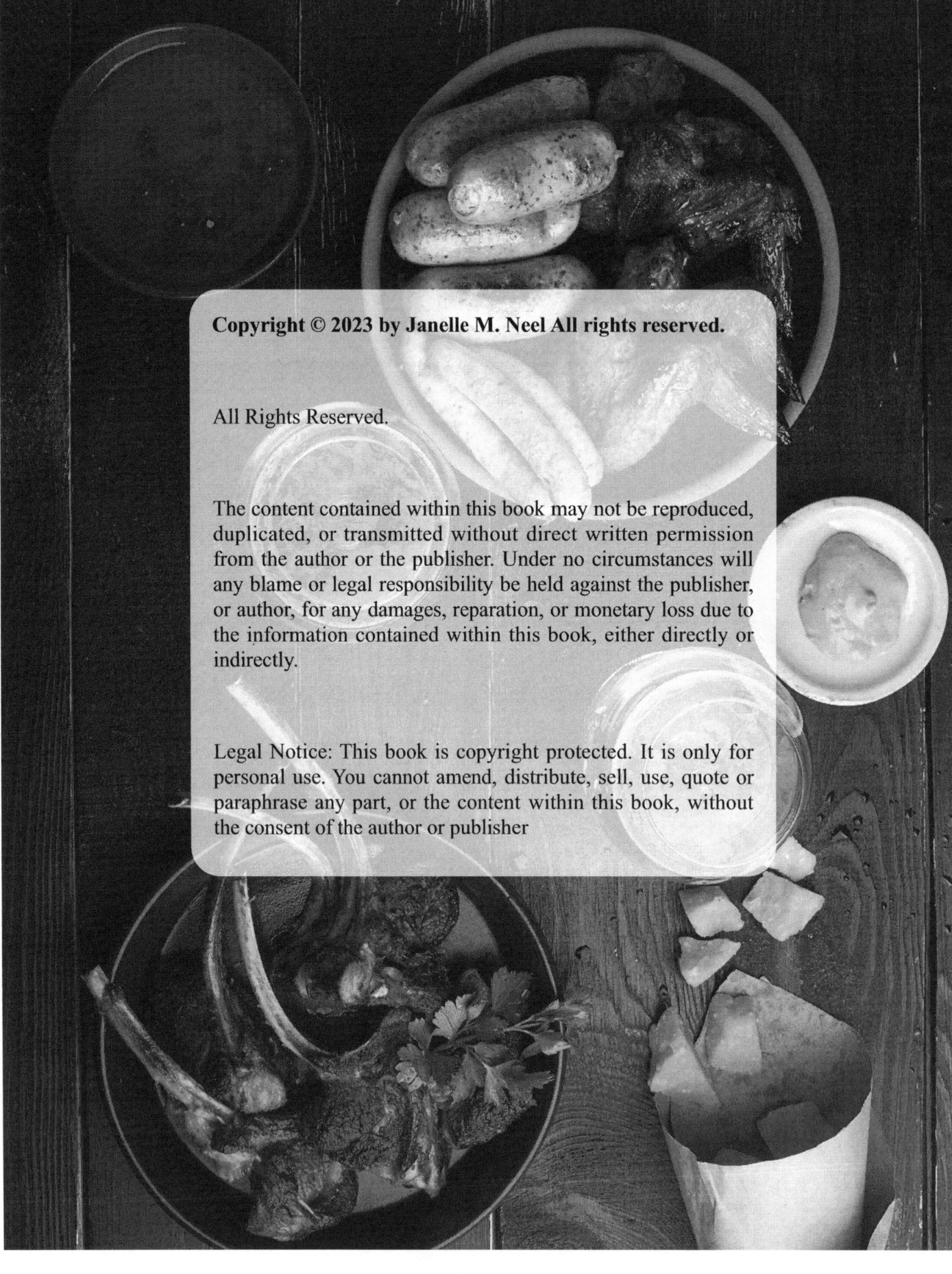

Copyright © 2023 by Janelle M. Neel All rights reserved.

All Rights Reserved.

The content contained within this book may not be reproduced, duplicated, or transmitted without direct written permission from the author or the publisher. Under no circumstances will any blame or legal responsibility be held against the publisher, or author, for any damages, reparation, or monetary loss due to the information contained within this book, either directly or indirectly.

Legal Notice: This book is copyright protected. It is only for personal use. You cannot amend, distribute, sell, use, quote or paraphrase any part, or the content within this book, without the consent of the author or publisher

CONTENTS

Introduction 6
   Understanding Diabetes 6
   Types of Diabetes 7
   Can Diabetics Eat Air Fried Food? 7
   What Foods Should People with Diabetes Avoid? 7

Measurement Conversions 8

Breakfast Recipes 10
   Cornbread 11
   Muffins Sandwich 11
   Tofu Scramble 12
   Blueberry Buns 12
   Breakfast Cheese Bread Cups 13
   Garlic Bread 13
   Breakfast Muffins 13
   Breakfast Pizza 14
   Cinnamon And Cheese Pancake 14
   Blueberry Muffins 14
   Sweet Nuts Butter 15
   Cauliflower Potato Mash 15
   Cauliflower Hash Browns 15
   Fried Egg 16
   Baked Eggs 16
   Tortilla 16
   Santa Fe Style Pizza 17
   Pancakes 17
   Zucchini And Walnut Cake With Maple Flavor Icing 18
   Air Fryer Scrambled Egg 18
   Scotch Eggs 19
   French Toast In Sticks 19
   Cocotte Eggs 20
   Morning Mini Cheeseburger Sliders 20
   Air Fried Sausage 20
   Avocado Taco Fry 21
   Zucchini Bread 21
   Peanut Butter & Banana Breakfast Sandwich 22
   Bruschetta 22
   Broccoli Mash 22

Appetizers And Siders Recipes 23

Vegetable Spring Rolls 24
Garlic & Cheese Potatoes 24
Air Fryer Crisp Egg Cups 25
Air Fryer Avocado Fries 25
Charred Bell Peppers 25
Honey Chili Chicken 26
Zucchini Fritters 26
Salmon Fries 27
Mini Popovers 27
Balsamic Cabbage 27
Green Beans 28
Cheesy Bell Pepper Eggs 28
Creamy Fennel 28
Spinach And Artichokes Sauté 29
Nutella Smores 29
Fried Garlic Green Tomatoes 29
Avocado Egg Rolls 30
Air Fried Cheesy Chicken Omelet 30
Air Fryer Buffalo Cauliflower 30
Air Fryer Roasted Corn 31
Onion Rings 31
Roasted Peanut Butter Squash 32
Brussels Sprouts 32
Air Fryer Egg Rolls 32
Cherry Pies 33
Zucchini Gratin 33
Kale And Walnuts 34
Fish Club Sandwich 34
Crispy Air Fryer Brussels Sprouts 35
Herbed Radish Sauté 35

Poultry Recipes 36

Lemon Pepper Chicken Breast 37
Buttermilk Chicken In Air-fryer 37
Breaded Chicken With Seed Chips 38
Crispy Chicken Thighs 38
Jerk Style Chicken Wings 38
Air Fried Blackened Chicken Breast 39
Crispy Ranch Air Fryer Nuggets 39
Orange Chicken Wings 40
Southwest Chicken In Air Fryer 40
Air Fried Maple Chicken Thighs 41
Chicken Wings 41
Buttermilk Fried Chicken 42
Mushroom Oatmeal 42

Air Fryer Chicken Cheese Quesadilla ... 43
Garlic-roasted Chicken With Creamer Potatoes ... 43
Chicken Cheesey Quesadilla In Air Fryer ... 43
Fried Lemon Chicken ... 44
Air Fryer Pork Chop & Broccoli ... 44
Ham And Cheese Stuffed Chicken Burgers ... 45
Lemon Chicken With Basil ... 45
Buffalo Chicken Hot Wings ... 46
Lemon Rosemary Chicken ... 46
Garlic Parmesan Chicken Tenders ... 47
Pork Rind Nachos ... 47
Breaded Chicken Tenderloins ... 47
Chicken Skewers With Yogurt ... 48
Tasty Chicken Tenders ... 48
Chicken Sandwich ... 49
Jamaican Jerk Pork In Air Fryer ... 49
Popcorn Chicken In Air Fryer ... 50

Beef, Pork And Lamb Recipes ... 51

Herbed Lamb Chops ... 52
Fish And Vegetable Tacos ... 52
Short Ribs ... 53
Warm Chicken And Spinach Salad ... 53
Cinnamon Spiced Popcorn ... 53
Pork Loin ... 54
Air Fried Empanadas ... 54
Chicken In Tomato Juice ... 55
Spicy Lamb Sirloin Steak ... 55
Asian Swordfish ... 56
Pork On A Blanket ... 56
Homemade Flamingos ... 56
Nutty Chicken Nuggets ... 57
Double Cheeseburger ... 57
Chicken Meatballs ... 58
Chocolate Chip Muffins ... 58
Pork Chops ... 59
Tuna Wraps ... 59
Meatloaf Slider Wraps ... 60
Pork Fillets With Serrano Ham ... 60
Fried Pork Chops ... 61
Stuffed Cabbage And Pork Loin Rolls ... 61
Marinated Loin Potatoes ... 61
Pork Belly ... 62
Strawberry Lime Pudding ... 62
Mustard-crusted Fish Fillets ... 63
Mediterranean Lamb Meatballs ... 63
Grilled Chicken ... 64

Diabetic Air Fryer Cookbook

Air Fryer Beef Empanadas ... 64
Steak ... 64

Fish And Seafood Recipes ... 65

Catfish With Green Beans, In Southern Style ... 66
Crab Cake ... 66
Frozen Shrimp With Crispy Coconut ... 67
Fish With Maille Dijon Originale Mustard ... 67
Air-fried Crumbed Fish ... 67
Salmon Cakes In Air Fryer ... 68
Salmon Patties ... 68
Lime-garlic Shrimp Kebabs ... 68
Parmesan Garlic Crusted Salmon ... 69
Air Fryer Salmon With Maple Soy Glaze ... 69
Garlic Rosemary Grilled Prawns ... 69
Lemon Pepper Shrimp In Air Fryer ... 70
Juicy Air Fryer Salmon ... 70
Grilled Salmon With Lemon ... 70
Parmesan Shrimp ... 71
Air Fryer Salmon Fillets ... 71
Air Fryer Lemon Cod ... 72
Honey & Sriracha Tossed Calamari ... 72
Cilantro Lime Shrimps ... 73
Salmon With Brown Sugar Glaze ... 73
Scallops With Creamy Tomato Sauce ... 74
Crispy Fish Sticks In Air Fryer ... 74
Air Fryer Crab Cakes ... 75
Celery Leaves And Garlic-oil Grilled ... 75
Fish Sticks ... 76
Roasted Salmon With Fennel Salad ... 76
Basil-parmesan Crusted Salmon ... 77
Shrimp Scampi ... 77
Air Fried Cajun Salmon ... 78
Salmon Cakes ... 78

Other Favorite Recipes ... 79

Zucchini Turkey Burgers ... 80
Roasted Potatoes ... 80
Tilapia With Coconut Rice ... 81
Creamy Halibut ... 81
Whole Wheat And Honey Pizza Dough ... 82
Air Fryer Tofu ... 82
Black Bean Salad With Grilled Pork Cutlets ... 83
Chicken Cheese Fillet ... 83
Beef Fajitas ... 84
One-skillet Italian Sausage Pasta ... 84

Turkey Cobb Salad 85
Almond-crusted Salmon 85
Recipe For Eight Flourless Brownies 86
Brown Rice & Lentil Salad 86
Air Fryer Brussels Sprouts 87
Potato Wedges 87
Quick Fry Chicken With Cauliflower And Water Chestnuts 88
Turkey And Zucchini Burgers With Corn On The Cob 88
Chicken Kebabs With Pistachio Gremolata 89
Cilantro Lime Quinoa 89
Air-fried Asparagus 90
Air Fried Fish And Chips 90
Lemony Yogurt Pound Cake 91
Chicken & Veggie Bowl With Brown Rice 91
Unstuffed Cabbage 92
Roasted Broccoli With Cheese Sauce 92
Italian Pork Chops 93
Macaroni And Cheese Recipe 93
Mashed Butternut Squash 94
Air Fried Artichoke Hearts 94

28 Day Meal Plan 95

Appendix : Recipes Index 97

INTRODUCTION

Diabetes mellitus, popularly referred to as just Diabetes, is a chronic condition that causes a person's blood glucose to become too high.

As a matter of fact, here you will find how to prevent and curb the disease, whether you have prediabetes or type 2 diabetes. My name is Janelle M. Neel, My first resolution after the type 2 diabetes diagnosis last year was to reform my diet fully. One of my biggest concerns was how to adjust my cooking practices. And to fast-track my new diabetes lifestyle, the first recommendation was the best air fryer for diabetics . Will an air fryer help a diabetic? It's a commonly asked question.

In short, an air fryer is not a miracle cure for diabetes. However, it can help you improve your diet as a diabetic and prepare food with less oil. If you are reading this page, it means that you have already decided to start a better Lifestyle. This book contains 1800 diabetes recipes simplify meal planning for individuals who live with diabetes. They allow home cooks to focus on cooking instead of research.

If you don't know how to start this new diet pattern, you might as well try the 28-Day meal plan in the cookbook first. After trying it, I believe you will love this healthy and simple diet.

Are you ready?

Let's dive right into it.

Understanding Diabetes

Diabetes is a chronic medical condition in which the body is unable to properly regulate the amount of sugar in the blood. It is caused by either a lack of insulin production or an inability of the body to properly use the insulin it produces.

Insulin is a hormone produced by the pancreas that helps the body to use glucose, or sugar, for energy. When the body does not produce enough insulin or is unable to use it properly, glucose builds up in the blood instead of being used for energy. This can lead to a variety of health problems, including heart disease, stroke, kidney disease, nerve damage, and vision loss.

Diabetes can be managed through lifestyle changes, such as eating a healthy diet and exercising regularly, as well as through medications and insulin therapy.

Types of Diabetes

There are two main types of diabetes: Type 1 and Type 2.

Type 1 diabetes is an autoimmune disorder in which the body's immune system attacks and destroys the cells in the pancreas that produce insulin. This type of diabetes usually develops in childhood or adolescence and requires lifelong insulin therapy.

Type 2 diabetes is the most common form of diabetes and is caused by a combination of lifestyle factors, such as poor diet and lack of exercise, and genetic factors. It is characterized by the body's inability to properly use the insulin it produces. This type of diabetes can often be managed through lifestyle changes, such as eating a healthy diet and exercising regularly, as well as through medications and insulin therapy.

Can Diabetics Eat Air Fried Food?

People with diabetes can eat air-fried foods, as they are lower in calories and fat than traditional fried foods.

Air-fried foods are cooked using hot air instead of oil, which helps to reduce the amount of fat and calories in the food. Additionally, air-fried foods are often lower in carbohydrates, which can help to keep blood sugar levels in check.

The most important thing is that people with diabetes should still focus on eating a balanced diet that includes plenty of fruits, vegetables, whole grains, and lean proteins.

What Foods Should People with Diabetes Avoid?

People with diabetes should avoid foods that are high in sugar, such as candy, cakes, cookies, and other sweets.

They should also limit their intake of processed foods, such as white bread, white rice, and other refined grains, as these can cause blood sugar levels to spike.

Additionally, people with diabetes should avoid foods that are high in saturated fat, such as red meat, full-fat dairy products, and fried foods. Alcohol should also be avoided, as it can interfere with blood sugar control.

Measurement Conversions

BASIC KITCHEN CONVERSIONS & EQUIVALENTS

DRY MEASUREMENTS CONVERSION CHART

3 TEASPOONS = 1 TABLESPOON = 1/16 CUP

6 TEASPOONS = 2 TABLESPOONS = 1/8 CUP

12 TEASPOONS = 4 TABLESPOONS = 1/4 CUP

24 TEASPOONS = 8 TABLESPOONS = 1/2 CUP

36 TEASPOONS = 12 TABLESPOONS = 3/4 CUP

48 TEASPOONS = 16 TABLESPOONS = 1 CUP

METRIC TO US COOKING CONVERSIONS

OVEN TEMPERATURES

120 °C = 250 °F

160 °C = 320 °F

180° C = 350 °F

205 °C = 400 °F

220 °C = 425 °F

LIQUID MEASUREMENTS CONVERSION CHART

8 FLUID OUNCES = 1 CUP = 1/2 PINT = 1/4 QUART

16 FLUID OUNCES = 2 CUPS = 1 PINT = 1/2 QUART

32 FLUID OUNCES = 4 CUPS = 2 PINTS = 1 QUART = 1/4 GALLON

128 FLUID OUNCES = 16 CUPS = 8 PINTS = 4 QUARTS = 1 GALLON

BAKING IN GRAMS

1 CUP FLOUR = 140 GRAMS

1 CUP SUGAR = 150 GRAMS

1 CUP POWDERED SUGAR = 160 GRAMS

1 CUP HEAVY CREAM = 235 GRAMS

VOLUME

1 MILLILITER = 1/5 TEASPOON

5 ML = 1 TEASPOON

15 ML = 1 TABLESPOON

240 ML = 1 CUP OR 8 FLUID OUNCES

1 LITER = 34 FL. OUNCES

WEIGHT

1 GRAM = .035 OUNCES

100 GRAMS = 3.5 OUNCES

500 GRAMS = 1.1 POUNDS

1 KILOGRAM = 35 OUNCES

US TO METRIC COOKING CONVERSIONS

1/5 TSP = 1 ML

1 TSP = 5 ML

1 TBSP = 15 ML

1 FL OUNCE = 30 ML

1 CUP = 237 ML

1 PINT (2 CUPS) = 473 ML

1 QUART (4 CUPS) = .95 LITER

1 GALLON (16 CUPS) = 3.8 LITERS

1 OZ = 28 GRAMS

1 POUND = 454 GRAMS

BUTTER

1 CUP BUTTER = 2 STICKS = 8 OUNCES = 230 GRAMS = 8 TABLESPOONS

WHAT DOES 1 CUP EQUAL

1 CUP = 8 FLUID OUNCES

1 CUP = 16 TABLESPOONS

1 CUP = 48 TEASPOONS

1 CUP = 1/2 PINT

1 CUP = 1/4 QUART

1 CUP = 1/16 GALLON

1 CUP = 240 ML

BAKING PAN CONVERSIONS

1 CUP ALL-PURPOSE FLOUR = 4.5 OZ

1 CUP ROLLED OATS = 3 OZ 1 LARGE EGG = 1.7 OZ

1 CUP BUTTER = 8 OZ 1 CUP MILK = 8 OZ

1 CUP HEAVY CREAM = 8.4 OZ

1 CUP GRANULATED SUGAR = 7.1 OZ

1 CUP PACKED BROWN SUGAR = 7.75 OZ

1 CUP VEGETABLE OIL = 7.7 OZ

1 CUP UNSIFTED POWDERED SUGAR = 4.4 OZ

BAKING PAN CONVERSIONS

9-INCH ROUND CAKE PAN = 12 CUPS

10-INCH TUBE PAN = 16 CUPS

11-INCH BUNDT PAN = 12 CUPS

9-INCH SPRINGFORM PAN = 10 CUPS

9 X 5 INCH LOAF PAN = 8 CUPS

9-INCH SQUARE PAN = 8 CUPS

Breakfast Recipes

Breakfast Recipes

Cornbread

Servings: 8 | Cooking Time: 25 Minutes

Ingredients:
- 3/4 cup almond flour
- 1 cup white cornmeal
- 1 tablespoon erythritol sweetener
- 1 1/2 teaspoons baking powder
- 1/4 teaspoon salt
- 1/2 teaspoon baking soda
- 6 tablespoons butter, unsalted; melted
- 2 eggs; beaten
- 1 1/2 cups buttermilk, low-fat

Directions:
1. Switch on the air fryer, insert fryer pan, grease it with olive oil, then shut with its lid, set the fryer at 360 degrees F and preheat for 5 minutes.
2. Meanwhile, crack the egg in a bowl and then whisk in butter and milk until blended.
3. Place flour in another bowl, add remaining ingredients, stir until well mixed and then stir in egg mixture until incorporated.
4. Open the fryer, pour the batter into the fryer pan, close with its lid and cook for 25 minutes at the 360 degrees F until nicely golden and crispy, shaking halfway through the frying.
5. When air fryer beeps, open its lid, take out the fryer pan, and then transfer the bread onto a serving plate.
6. Cut the bread into pieces and serve.

Nutrition Info:
- Calories: 138 CalCarbs: 25 gFat: 2 gProtein: 5 gFiber: 2 g

Muffins Sandwich

Servings: 1 | Cooking Time: 10 Minutes

Ingredients:
- Nonstick Spray Oil
- 1 slice of white cheddar cheese
- 1 slice of Canadian bacon
- 1 English muffin, divided
- 15 ml hot water
- 1 large egg
- Salt and pepper to taste

Directions:
1. Spray the inside of an 85g mold with oil spray and place it in the air fryer.
2. Preheat the air fryer, set it to 160°C.
3. Add the Canadian cheese and bacon in the preheated air fryer.
4. Pour the hot water and the egg into the hot pan and season with salt and pepper.
5. Select Bread, set to 10 minutes.
6. Take out the English muffins after 7 minutes, leaving the egg for the full time.
7. Build your sandwich by placing the cooked egg on top of the English muffing and serve

Nutrition Info:
- Calories 400 Fat 26g, Carbohydrates 26g, Sugar 15 g, Protein 3 g, Cholesterol 155 mg

Tofu Scramble

Servings: 3 | Cooking Time: 18 Minutes

Ingredients:
- 12 ounces tofu, extra-firm, drained, ½-inch cubed
- 1 teaspoon garlic powder
- 1 teaspoon onion powder
- 1 teaspoon paprika
- 1/2 teaspoon ground black pepper
- 1/2 teaspoon salt
- 1 tablespoon olive oil
- 2 teaspoon xanthan gum

Directions:
1. Switch on the air fryer, insert fryer basket, grease it with olive oil, then shut with its lid, set the fryer at 220 degrees F and preheat for 5 minutes.
2. Meanwhile, place tofu pieces in a bowl, drizzle with oil, and sprinkle with xanthan gum and toss until well coated.
3. Add remaining ingredients to the tofu and then toss until well coated.
4. Open the fryer, add tofu in it, close with its lid and cook for 13 minutes until nicely golden and crispy, shaking the basket every 5 minutes.
5. When air fryer beeps, open its lid, transfer tofu onto a serving plate and serve.

Nutrition Info:
- Calories: 94 CalCarbs: 5 gFat: 5 gProtein: 6 gFiber: 0 g

Blueberry Buns

Servings: 6 | Cooking Time: 12 Minutes

Ingredients:
- 240g all-purpose flour
- 50g granulated sugar
- 8g baking powder
- 2g of salt
- 85g chopped cold butter
- 85g of fresh blueberries
- 3g grated fresh ginger
- 113 ml whipping cream
- 2 large eggs
- 4 ml vanilla extract
- 5 ml of water

Directions:
1. Put sugar, flour, baking powder and salt in a large bowl.
2. Put the butter with the flour using a blender or your hands until the mixture resembles thick crumbs.
3. Mix the blueberries and ginger in the flour mixture and set aside
4. Mix the whipping cream, 1 egg and the vanilla extract in a different container.
5. Put the cream mixture with the flour mixture until combined.
6. Shape the dough until it reaches a thickness of approximately 38 mm and cut it into eighths.
7. Spread the buns with a combination of egg and water. Set aside Preheat the air fryer set it to 180°C.
8. Place baking paper in the preheated inner basket and place the buns on top of the paper. Cook for 12 minutes at 180°C, until golden brown

Nutrition Info:
- Calories: 105 Fat: 1.64g Carbohydrates: 20.09gProtein: 2.43g Sugar: 2.1g Cholesterol: 0mg

Breakfast Cheese Bread Cups

Servings: 2 | Cooking Time: 15 Minutes

Ingredients:
- 2 eggs
- 2 tbsps. Grated cheddar cheese
- Salt and pepper
- 1 ham slice cut into 2 pieces
- 4 bread slices flatted with a rolling pin

Directions:
1. Spray both sides of the ramekins with cooking spray.
2. Place two slices of bread into each ramekin.
3. Add the ham slice pieces into each ramekin. Crack an egg in each ramekin then sprinkle with cheese. Season with salt and pepper.
4. Place the ramekins into air fryer at 300°Fahrenheit for 15-minutes.
5. Serve warm.

Nutrition Info:
- Calories: 162 kcal Total Fat: 8g Carbs: 10g Protein: 11g

Garlic Bread

Servings: 5 | Cooking Time: 15 Minutes

Ingredients:
- 2 stale French rolls
- 4 tbsps. Crushed or crumpled garlic
- 1 cup mayonnaise
- Powdered grated Parmesan
- 1 tbsp. olive oil

Directions:
1. Preheat the air fryer to 200ºC for 5 minutes.
2. Mix mayonnaise with garlic and set aside.
3. Cut the baguettes into slices, but without separating them completely.
4. Fill the cavities of equals, then brush with olive oil and sprinkle with grated cheese.
5. Place in the basket of the air fryer. Cook for 10 minutes at 180ºC. Serve.

Nutrition Info:
- Calories: 151 kcal Fat: 7.1g Carbs: 17.9g Protein: 3.6g

Breakfast Muffins

Servings: 2 | Cooking Time: 6 Minutes

Ingredients:
- 2 whole-wheat English muffins
- 4 slices bacon
- Pepper
- 2 eggs

Directions:
1. Crack an egg each into ramekins then season with pepper.
2. Place the ramekins and bacon in your preheated air fryer at 390°F.
3. Allow to cook for 6-minutes with the bacon and muffins.
4. When the bacon and eggs are done cooking, add two pieces of bacon and one egg to each egg muffin. Serve when hot.

Nutrition Info:
- Calories: 276 kcal Total Fat: 12g Carbs: 10.2g Protein: 17.3g

Breakfast Pizza

Servings: 1-2 | Cooking Time: 8 Minutes

Ingredients:
- 10 ml of olive oil
- 1 prefabricated pizza dough (178 mm)
- 28g low moisture mozzarella cheese
- 2 slices smoked ham
- 1 egg
- 2g chopped cilantro

Directions:
1. Pass olive oil over the prefabricated pizza dough.
2. Add mozzarella cheese and smoked ham in the dough.
3. Preheat the air fryer, set it to 175°C.
4. Place the pizza in the preheated air fryer and cook for 8 minutes at 175°C.
5. Remove the baskets after 5 minutes and open the egg on the pizza.
6. Replace the baskets in the air fryer and finish cooking. Garnish with chopped coriander and serve.

Nutrition Info:
- Calories: 224 Fat: 7.5g Carbohydrates: 25.2g Protein: 14g Sugar: 0g Cholesterol: 13mg

Cinnamon And Cheese Pancake

Servings: 4 | Cooking Time: 20 Minutes

Ingredients:
- 2 eggs
- 2 cups reduced-fat cream cheese
- 1/2 tsp. cinnamon
- 1 pack Stevia

Directions:
1. Adjust the Air Fryer to 330ºF.
2. Mix the cream cheese, cinnamon, eggs, and stevia.
3. Pour 1/4 of the mixture into the Air fryer basket.
4. Cook for 2 minutes on all sides. Repeat the process with the remaining portion of the mixture. Serve.

Nutrition Info:
- Calories: 140 kcal Carbs: 5.4g Fat: 10.6g Protein: 22.7g

Blueberry Muffins

Servings: 14 | Cooking Time: 30 Minutes

Ingredients:
- 1 cup almond flour
- 1 cup frozen blueberries
- 2 teaspoons baking powder
- 1/3 cup erythritol sweetener
- 1 teaspoon vanilla extract, unsweetened
- ½ teaspoon salt
- ¼ cup melted coconut oil
- 1 egg, pastured
- ¼ cup applesauce, unsweetened
- ¼ cup almond milk, unsweetened

Directions:
1. Switch on the air fryer, insert fryer basket, grease it with olive oil, then shut with its lid, set the fryer at 360 degrees F and preheat for 10 minutes.
2. Meanwhile, place flour in a large bowl, add berries, salt, sweetener, and baking powder and stir until well combined.
3. Crack the eggs in another bowl, whisk in vanilla, milk, and applesauce until combined and then slowly whisk in flour mixture until incorporated.
4. Take fourteen silicone muffin cups, grease them with oil, and then evenly fill them with the prepared batter.
5. Open the fryer, stack muffin cups in it, close with its lid and cook for 10 minutes until muffins are nicely golden brown and set.
6. When air fryer beeps, open its lid, transfer muffins onto a serving plate and then remaining muffins in the same manner.
7. Serve straight away.

Nutrition Info:
- Calories: 201 CalCarbs: 27.3 gFat: 8.8 gProtein: 3 gFiber: 1.2 g

Sweet Nuts Butter

Servings: 5 | Cooking Time: 25 Minutes

Ingredients:
- 1½ pounds sweet potatoes, peeled and cut into ½ inch pieces (2 medium)
- ½ tbsp. olive oil
- 1 tbsp. melted butter
- 1 tbsp. finely chopped walnuts
- ½ tsp. grated one orange
- ⅛ tsp. nutmeg
- ⅛ tsp. ground cinnamon

Directions:
1. Put sweet potatoes in a small bowl and sprinkle with oil. Stir until covered and then pour into the basket, ensuring that they are in a single layer. Cook at a temperature of 350°F for 20 to 25 minutes, stirring or turning halfway through cooking. Remove them to the serving plate. Combine the butter, nuts, orange zest, nutmeg, and cinnamon in a small bowl and pour the mixture over the sweet potatoes.

Nutrition Info:
- Calories: 141 Fat: 1.01g Carbohydrates: 6.68g Protein: 1.08g Sugar: 0.25g Cholesterol: 7mg

Cauliflower Potato Mash

Servings: 4 | Cooking Time: 30 Minutes

Ingredients:
- 2 cups potatoes, peeled and cubed
- 2 tbsp. butter
- ¼ cup milk
- 10 oz. cauliflower florets
- ¾ tsp. salt

Directions:
1. Add water to the saucepan and bring to boil.
2. Reduce heat and simmer for 10 minutes.
3. Drain vegetables well. Transfer vegetables, butter, milk, and salt in a blender and blend until smooth.
4. Serve and enjoy.

Nutrition Info:
- Calories 128 Fat 6.2 g, Carbohydrates 16.3 g, Sugar 3.3 g, Protein 3.2 g, Cholesterol 17 mg

Cauliflower Hash Browns

Servings: 6 | Cooking Time: 25 Minutes

Ingredients:
- 1/4 cup chickpea flour
- 4 cups cauliflower rice
- 1/2 medium white onion, peeled and chopped
- 1/2 teaspoon garlic powder
- 1 tablespoon xanthan gum
- 1/2 teaspoon salt
- 1 tablespoon nutritional yeast flakes
- 1 teaspoon ground paprika

Directions:
1. Switch on the air fryer, insert fryer basket, grease it with olive oil, then shut with its lid, set the fryer at 375 degrees F and preheat for 10 minutes.
2. Meanwhile, place all the ingredients in a bowl, stir until well mixed and then shape the mixture into six rectangular disks, each about ½-inch thick.
3. Open the fryer, add hash browns in it in a single layer, close with its lid and cook for 25 minutes at the 375 degrees F until nicely golden and crispy, turning halfway through the frying.
4. When air fryer beeps, open its lid, transfer hash browns to a serving plate and serve.

Nutrition Info:
- Calories: 115.2 CalCarbs: 6.2 gFat: 7.3 gProtein: 7.4 gFiber: 2.2 g

Fried Egg

Servings: 1 | Cooking Time: 4 Minutes

Ingredients:
- 1 egg, pastured
- 1/8 teaspoon salt
- 1/8 teaspoon cracked black pepper

Directions:
1. Take the fryer pan, grease it with olive oil and then crack the egg in it.
2. Switch on the air fryer, insert fryer pan, then shut with its lid, and set the fryer at 370 degrees F.
3. Set the frying time to 3 minutes, then when the air fryer beep, open its lid and check the egg; if egg needs more cooking, then air fryer it for another minute.
4. Transfer the egg to a serving plate, season with salt and black pepper and serve.

Nutrition Info:
- Calories: 90 CalCarbs: 0.6 gFat: 7 gProtein: 6.3 gFiber: 0 g

Baked Eggs

Servings: 2 | Cooking Time: 17 Minutes

Ingredients:
- 2 tablespoons frozen spinach, thawed
- ½ teaspoon salt
- ¼ teaspoon ground black pepper
- 2 eggs, pastured
- 3 teaspoons grated parmesan cheese, reduced-fat
- 2 tablespoons milk, unsweetened, reduced-fat

Directions:
1. Switch on the air fryer, insert fryer basket, grease it with olive oil, then shut with its lid, set the fryer at 330 degrees F and preheat for 5 minutes.
2. Meanwhile, take two silicon muffin cups, grease them with oil, then crack an egg into each cup and evenly add cheese, spinach, and milk.
3. Season the egg with salt and black pepper and gently stir the ingredients, without breaking the egg yolk.
4. Open the fryer, add muffin cups in it, close with its lid and cook for 8 to 12 minutes until eggs have cooked to desired doneness.
5. When air fryer beeps, open its lid, take out the muffin cups and serve.

Nutrition Info:
- Calories: 161 CalCarbs: 3 gFat: 11.4 gProtein: 12.1 gFiber: 1.1 g

Tortilla

Servings: Two | Cooking Time: 20 Minutes

Ingredients:
- 2 eggs
- 2 slices of ham, chopped
- 2 slices of chopped mozzarella
- 1 tbsp. chopped onion soup
- ½ cup chopped parsley and chives tea
- Salt, black pepper and oregano to taste
- Olive oil spread

Directions:
1. Preheat the air fryer for the time of 5 minutes and the temperature at 200C.
2. Spread a refractory that fits in the basket of the air fryer and has a high shelf and reserve.
3. In a bowl, beat the eggs lightly with a fork. Add the fillings and spices. Place the refractory container in the basket of the air fryer and pour the beaten eggs being careful not to fall.
4. Set the time from 10 to 15 minutes and press the power button. The tortilla is ready when it is golden brown

Nutrition Info:
- Calories: 41 Fat: 1.01g Carbohydrates: 6.68g Protein: 1.08g Sugar: 0.25g Cholesterol: 0mg

Santa Fe Style Pizza

Servings: Two | Cooking Time: 10 Minutes

Ingredients:
- 1 tsp. vegetable oil
- ½ tsp. ground cumin
- 2 tortillas 7 to 8 inches in diameter
- ¼ cup black bean sauce prepared
- 4 ounces cooked chicken, in strips or grated
- 1 tbsp. taco seasonings
- 2 tbsp. prepared chipotle sauce, or preferred sauce
- ¼ cup plus 2 tbsp. corn kernels, fresh or frozen (thawed)
- 1 tbsp. sliced scallions
- 1 tsp. chopped cilantro
- ⅔ cup grated pepper jack cheese

Directions:
1. Put the oil with the cumin in a small bowl; spread the mixture on both tortillas. Then spread the black bean sauce evenly over both tortillas. Put the chicken pieces and taco seasonings in medium bowl; Stir until chicken is covered. Add the sauce and mix it with the covered chicken.
2. Remove half of the chicken and place it over the bean sauce in one of the tortillas. Put half the corn, chives, and cilantro over the tortilla and then cover with half the cheese. Put the pizza inside the basket and cook it at a temperature of 400°F for 10 minutes. Prepare the other tortilla and cook it after removing the first one.

Nutrition Info:
- Calories: 41 Fat: 1.01g Carbohydrates: 6.68g Protein: 1.08g Sugar: 0.25g Cholesterol: 0mg

Pancakes

Servings: 4 | Cooking Time: 29 Minutes

Ingredients:
- 1 1/2 cup coconut flour
- 1 teaspoon salt
- 3 1/2 teaspoons baking powder
- 1 tablespoon erythritol sweetener
- 1 1/2 teaspoon baking soda
- 3 tablespoons melted butter
- 1 1/4 cups milk, unsweetened, reduced-fat
- 1 egg, pastured

Directions:
1. Switch on the air fryer, insert fryer pan, grease it with olive oil, then shut with its lid, set the fryer at 220 degrees F and preheat for 5 minutes.
2. Meanwhile, take a medium bowl, add all the ingredients in it, whisk until well blended and then let the mixture rest for 5 minutes.
3. Open the fryer, pour in some of the pancake mixture as thin as possible, close with its lid and cook for 6 minutes until nicely golden, turning the pancake halfway through the frying.
4. When air fryer beeps, open its lid, transfer pancake onto a serving plate and use the remaining batter for cooking more pancakes in the same manner.
5. Serve straight away with fresh fruits slices.

Nutrition Info:
- Calories: 237.7 CalCarbs: 39.2 gFat: 10.2 gProtein: 6.3 gFiber: 1.3 g

Zucchini And Walnut Cake With Maple Flavor Icing

Servings: 5 | Cooking Time: 35 Minutes

Ingredients:
- 1 9-ounce package of yellow cake mix
- 1 egg
- ⅓ cup of water
- ½ cup grated zucchini
- ¼ cup chopped walnuts
- ¾ tsp. of cinnamon
- ¼ tsp. nutmeg
- ¼ tsp. ground ginger
- Maple Flavor Glaze

Directions:
1. Preheat the fryer to a temperature of 350°F. Prepare an 8 x 3⅞ inch loaf pan. Prepare the cake dough according to package directions, using ⅓ cup of water instead of ½ cup. Add zucchini, nuts, cinnamon, nutmeg, and ginger.
2. Pour the dough into the prepared mold and put it inside the basket. Bake until a toothpick inserted in the middle of the cake is clean when removed for 32 to 34 minutes.
3. Remove the cake from the fryer and let it cool on a grill for 10 minutes. Then, remove the cake and place it on a serving plate. Stop cooling just warm. Spray it with maple flavor glaze.

Nutrition Info:
- Calories: 196 Carbohydrates: 27gFat: 11g Protein: 1g Sugar: 7g Cholesterol: 0mg

Air Fryer Scrambled Egg

Servings: 2 | Cooking Time: 10 Minutes

Ingredients:
- 2 eggs
- 1 chopped tomato
- Dash of salt
- 1 tsp. butter
- 1/4 cup cream

Directions:
1. Put the eggs in a bowl then add salt and the cream. Whisk until fluffy.
2. Adjust the air fryer to 300°F.
3. Add butter to baking pan and place it into the preheated air fryer.
4. Add the egg mixture to the baking pan once the butter has melted.
5. Cook for 10-minutes. Serve warm.

Nutrition Info:
- Calories: 105 kcal Carbs: 2.3g Fat: 8g Protein: 6.4g

Scotch Eggs

Servings: 4 | Cooking Time: 15 Minutes

Ingredients:
- 1-pound pork sausage, pastured
- 2 tablespoons chopped parsley
- 1/8 teaspoon salt
- 1/8 teaspoon grated nutmeg
- 1 tablespoon chopped chives
- 1/8 teaspoon ground black pepper
- 2 teaspoons ground mustard, and more as needed
- 4 eggs, hard-boiled, shell peeled
- 1 cup shredded parmesan cheese, low-fat

Directions:
1. Switch on the air fryer, insert fryer basket, grease it with olive oil, then shut with its lid, set the fryer at 400 degrees F and preheat for 10 minutes.
2. Meanwhile, place sausage in a bowl, add salt, black pepper, parsley, chives, nutmeg, and mustard, then stir until well mixed and shape the mixture into four patties.
3. Peel each boiled egg, then place an egg on a patty and shape the meat around it until the egg has evenly covered.
4. Place cheese in a shallow dish, and then roll the egg in the cheese until covered completely with cheese; prepare remaining eggs in the same manner.
5. Then open the fryer, add eggs in it, close with its lid and cook for 15 minutes at the 400 degrees F until nicely golden and crispy, turning the eggs and spraying with oil halfway through the frying.
6. When air fryer beeps, open its lid, transfer eggs onto a serving plate and serve with mustard.

Nutrition Info:
- Calories: 533 CalCarbs: 2 gFat: 43 gProtein: 33 gFiber: 1 g

French Toast In Sticks

Servings: 4 | Cooking Time: 10 Minutes

Ingredients:
- 4 slices of white bread, 38 mm thick, preferably hard
- 2 eggs
- 60 ml of milk
- 15 ml maple sauce
- 2 ml vanilla extract
- Nonstick Spray Oil
- 38g of sugar
- 3ground cinnamon
- Maple syrup, to serve
- Sugar to sprinkle

Directions:
1. Cut each slice of bread into thirds making 12 pieces. Place sideways
2. Beat the eggs, milk, maple syrup and vanilla.
3. Preheat the air fryer, set it to 175°C.
4. Dip the sliced bread in the egg mixture and place it in the preheated air fryer. Sprinkle French toast generously with oil spray.
5. Cook French toast for 10 minutes at 175°C. Turn the toast halfway through cooking.
6. Mix the sugar and cinnamon in a bowl.
7. Cover the French toast with the sugar and cinnamon mixture when you have finished cooking.
8. Serve with Maple syrup and sprinkle with powdered sugar

Nutrition Info:
- Calories 128 Fat 6.2 g, Carbohydrates 16.3 g, Sugar 3.3 g, Protein 3.2 g, Cholesterol 17 mg

Cocotte Eggs

Servings: 1 | Cooking Time: 15 Minutes

Ingredients:
- 1 tbsp. olive oil soup
- 2 tbsp. crumbly ricotta
- 1 tbsp. parmesan cheese soup
- 1 slice of gorgonzola cheese
- 1 slice of Brie cheese
- 1 tbsp. cream soup
- 1 egg
- Nutmeg and salt to taste
- Butternut to taste

Directions:
1. Spread with olive oil in the bottom of a small glass refractory. Place the cheese in the bottom and season with nutmeg and salt. Add the cream.
2. Break the egg into a cup and gently add it to the refractory mixture.
3. Preheat the air fryer for the time of 5 minutes and the temperature at 200C. Put the refractory in the basket of the air fryer, set the time to 10 minutes, and press the power button. Remove and serve still hot.

Nutrition Info:
- Calories: 138 Cal Carbs: 3 g Fat: 33 g Protein: 7.4 g Fiber: 2.2 g

Morning Mini Cheeseburger Sliders

Servings: 6 | Cooking Time: 10minutes

Ingredients:
- 1 lb. ground beef
- 6 slices cheddar cheese
- 6 dinner rolls
- Salt and Black pepper

Directions:
1. Adjust the air fryer to 390°F.
2. Form 6 beef patties (each about 5 oz.) and season with salt and black pepper.
3. Add the burger patties to the cooking basket and cook them for 10 minutes.
4. Place bun and the cheese and cook for another minute.

Nutrition Info:
- Calories: 262 kcal Total Fat: 9.4g Carbs: 8.2g Protein: 16.2g

Air Fried Sausage

Servings: 2 | Cooking Time: 14 Minutes

Ingredients:
- 2-3 thick sausages

Directions:
1. Preheat air fryer to 360 degrees.
2. Pierce the sausage skin with a fork.
3. Put the sausage in the air fryer and cook for 12 to 15 minutes. After about 6 minutes, give the fryer tray a good shake to prevent overcooking in any area.
4. Serve with eggs or cut up to use in another recipe.

Nutrition Info:
- Calories: 106 kcal Carbs: 10g Fat: 3.2g Protein: 9g

Avocado Taco Fry

Servings: 12 Slices | Cooking Time: 20 Minutes

Ingredients:
- 1 peeled avocado, sliced
- 1 beaten egg
- 1/2 cup panko bread crumbs
- Salt
- Tortillas and toppings

Directions:
1. Using a bowl, add in the egg.
2. Using a separate bowl, set in the breadcrumbs.
3. Dip the avocado into the bowl with the beaten egg and coat with the breadcrumbs. Sprinkle the coated wedges with a bit of salt.
4. Arrange them in the cooking basket in a single layer.
5. Set the Air Fryer to 392 degrees and cook for 15 minutes. Shake the basket halfway through the cooking process.

Nutrition Info:
- Calorie: 140 kcal Carbs: 12g Fat: 8.8g Protein: 6g

Zucchini Bread

Servings: 8 | Cooking Time: 40 Minutes

Ingredients:
- ¾ cup shredded zucchini
- 1/2 cup almond flour
- 1/4 teaspoon salt
- 1/4 cup cocoa powder, unsweetened
- 1/2 cup chocolate chips, unsweetened, divided
- 6 tablespoons erythritol sweetener
- 1/2 teaspoon baking soda
- 2 tablespoons olive oil
- 1/2 teaspoon vanilla extract, unsweetened
- 2 tablespoons butter, unsalted, melted
- 1 egg, pastured

Directions:
1. Switch on the air fryer, insert fryer basket, grease it with olive oil, then shut with its lid, set the fryer at 310 degrees F and preheat for 10 minutes.
2. Meanwhile, place flour in a bowl, add salt, cocoa powder, and baking soda and stir until mixed.
3. Crack the eggs in another bowl, whisk in sweetener, egg, oil, butter, and vanilla until smooth and then slowly whisk in flour mixture until incorporated.
4. Add zucchini along with 1/3 cup chocolate chips and then fold until just mixed.
5. Take a mini loaf pan that fits into the air fryer, grease it with olive oil, then pour in the prepared batter and sprinkle remaining chocolate chips on top.
6. Open the fryer, place the loaf pan in it, close with its lid and cook for 30 minutes at the 310 degrees F until inserted toothpick into the bread slides out clean.
7. When air fryer beeps, open its lid, remove the loaf pan, then place it on a wire rack and let the bread cool in it for 20 minutes.
8. Take out the bread, let it cool completely, then cut it into slices and serve.

Nutrition Info:
- Calories: 356 CalCarbs: 49 gFat: 17 gProtein: 5.1 gFiber: 2.5 g

Peanut Butter & Banana Breakfast Sandwich

Servings: 1 | Cooking Time: 6 Minutes

Ingredients:
- 2 slices whole-wheat bread
- 1 tsp. sugar-free maple syrup
- 1 sliced banana
- 2 tbsps. Peanut butter

Directions:
1. Evenly coat each side of the sliced bread with peanut butter.
2. Add the sliced banana and drizzle with some sugar-free maple syrup.
3. Adjust the air fryer to 330°F then cook for 6 minutes. Serve warm.

Nutrition Info:
- Calories: 211 kcal Total Fat: 8.2g Carbs: 6.3g Protein: 11.2g

Bruschetta

Servings: 2 | Cooking Time: 10 Minutes

Ingredients:
- 4 slices of Italian bread
- 1 cup chopped tomato tea
- 1 cup grated mozzarella tea
- Olive oil
- Oregano, salt, and pepper
- 4 fresh basil leaves

Directions:
1. Preheat the air fryer. Set the timer of 5 minutes and the temperature to 2000C.
2. Sprinkle the slices of Italian bread with olive oil. Divide the chopped tomatoes and mozzarella between the slices. Season with salt, pepper, and oregano.
3. Put oil in the filling. Place a basil leaf on top of each slice.
4. Put the bruschetta in the basket of the air fryer being careful not to spill the filling. Set the timer of 5 minutes, set the temperature to 180C, and press the power button.
5. Transfer the bruschetta to a plate and serve.

Nutrition Info:
- Calories: 434 Fat: 14g Carbohydrates: 63g Protein: 11g Sugar: 8g Cholesterol: 0mg

Broccoli Mash

Servings: 4 | Cooking Time: 20-30 Minutes

Ingredients:
- 20 oz. Broccoli florets
- 3 oz. Butter; melted
- 1 garlic clove; minced
- 4 tbsp. Basil; chopped.
- A drizzle of olive oil
- A pinch of salt and black pepper

Directions:
1. Take a bowl and mix the broccoli with the oil, salt and pepper, toss and transfer to your air fryer's basket.
2. Cook at 380°f for 20 minutes, cool the broccoli down and put it in a blender
3. Add the rest of the ingredients, pulse, divide the mash between plates and serve as a side dish.

Nutrition Info:
- Calories: 200 Fat: 14g Fiber: 3g Carbs: 6g Protein: 7g

Appetizers And Siders Recipes

Appetizers And Siders Recipes

Vegetable Spring Rolls

Servings: 4 | Cooking Time: 15 Minutes

Ingredients:
- Toasted sesame seeds
- Large carrots – grated
- Spring roll wrappers
- One egg white
- Gluten-free soy sauce, a dash
- Half cabbage: sliced
- Olive oil: 2 tbsp.

Directions:
1. In a pan over high flame heat, 2 tbsp. of oil and sauté the chopped vegetables. Then add soy sauce. Do not overcook the vegetables.
2. Turn off the heat and add toasted sesame seeds.
3. Lay spring roll wrappers flat on a surface and add egg white with a brush on the sides.
4. Add some vegetable mix in the wrapper and fold.
5. Spray the spring rolls with oil spray and air dry for 8 minutes at 200 C.
6. Serve with dipping sauce.

Nutrition Info:
- 129 calories| fat 16.3g |carbohydrates 8.2g |protein 12.1 g

Garlic & Cheese Potatoes

Servings: 4 | Cooking Time: 40 Minutes

Ingredients:
- halved Idaho baking potatoes
- 1 tbsp. garlic powder
- Salt
- ½ cup shredded cheddar cheese
- 1 tsp. parsley

Directions:
1. Toss all your ingredients in a bowl except cheese.
2. Place potatoes in a baking dish and sprinkle cheese over top of them.
3. Set in the air fryers and cook for 40 minutes at 390°F.

Nutrition Info:
- Calories: 498 kcal; Fat: 19.09g; Carbs: 67.27g; Protein: 16.5g

Air Fryer Crisp Egg Cups

Servings: 4 | Cooking Time: 10 Minutes

Ingredients:
- Toasted bread: 4 slices (whole-wheat)
- Cooking spray, nonstick
- Large eggs: 4
- Margarine: 1 and a half tbsp. (trans-fat free)
- Ham: 1 slice
- Salt: 1/8 tsp
- Black pepper: 1/8 tsp

Directions:
1. Let the air fryer Preheat to 375 F, with the air fryer basket.
2. Take four ramekins, spray with cooking spray.
3. Trim off the crusts from bread, add margarine to one side.
4. Put the bread down, into a ramekin, margarine-side in.
5. Press it in the cup. Cut the ham in strips, half-inch thick, and add on top of the bread.
6. Add one egg to the ramekins. Add salt and pepper.
7. Put the custard cups in the air fryer. Air fry at 375 F for 10–13 minutes.
8. Remove the ramekin from the air fryer and serve.

Nutrition Info:
- Calories 150|Total Fat 8g|Total Carbohydrate 6g Protein 12g

Air Fryer Avocado Fries

Servings: 2 | Cooking Time: 10 Minutes

Ingredients:
- One avocado
- One egg
- Whole wheat bread crumbs: 1/2 cup
- Salt: 1/2 teaspoon

Directions:
1. Avocado should be firm and firm. Cut into wedges.
2. In a bowl, beat egg with salt. In another bowl, add the crumbs.
3. Coat wedges in egg, then in crumbs.
4. Air fry them at 400F for 8-10 minutes. Toss halfway through.
5. Serve hot.

Nutrition Info:
- Calories: 251kcal | Carbohydrates: 19g | Protein: 6g | Fat: 17g |

Charred Bell Peppers

Servings: 3 | Cooking Time: 5 Minutes

Ingredients:
- 20 bells sliced and seeded peppers.
- 1 tsp. olive oil
- Sea salt
- 1 lemon

Directions:
1. Preheat your air fryer to 390°F.
2. Sprinkle the peppers with oil and salt.
3. Cook the peppers in the air fryer for 4 minutes.
4. Place peppers in a large bowl, and squeeze lemon juice over the top.
5. Season with salt and pepper. Serve.

Nutrition Info:
- Calories: 30 kcal; Fat: 0.25g; Carbs: 6.91g; Protein: 1.28g

Honey Chili Chicken

Servings: 3 | Cooking Time: 15 Minutes

Ingredients:
- For chicken fingers:
- 1 lb. chicken
- 2 ½- tsp. ginger-garlic paste
- 1 tsp. red chili sauce
- ¼- tsp. salt
- ¼- tsp. red chili powder
- Edible orange food coloring
- For sauce:
- 2 tbsp. olive oil
- 1 capsicum
- 2 small onions
- 1 ½- tsp. ginger garlic paste
- ½- tbsp. red chili sauce
- 2 tbsp. tomato ketchup
- 1 ½- tbsp. sweet chili sauce
- 2 tsp. soy sauce
- 2 tsp. vinegar
- 1-2 tbsp. honey
- A pinch of black pepper
- 2 tsp. red chili flakes

Directions:
1. Blend all of the components for the marinade and marinate veal fingers for 30 minutes.
2. Blend the breadcrumbs, oregano and red chili flakes and add the marinated fingers on this mix.
3. Preheat the Air Fryer to 160 F and cook for 15 minutes, shaking the fry basket occasionally.

Nutrition Info:
- Calories 295 Fat 17 g Carbohydrates 4 g Sugar 0.1 g Protein 29 g Cholesterol 260 mg

Zucchini Fritters

Servings: 4 | Cooking Time: 12 Minutes

Ingredients:
- 2 medium zucchinis, ends trimmed
- 3 tablespoons almond flour
- 1 tablespoon salt
- 1 teaspoon garlic powder
- ¼ teaspoon paprika
- ¼ teaspoon ground black pepper
- ¼ teaspoon onion powder
- 1 egg, pastured

Directions:
1. Wash and pat dry the zucchini, then cut its ends and grate the zucchini.
2. Place grated zucchini in a colander, sprinkle with salt and let it rest for 10 minutes.
3. Then wrap zucchini in a kitchen cloth and squeeze moisture from it as much as possible and place dried zucchini in another bowl.
4. Add remaining ingredients into the zucchini and then stir until mixed.
5. Take fryer basket, line it with parchment paper, grease it with oil and drop zucchini mixture on it by a spoonful, about 1-inch apart and then spray well with oil.
6. Switch on the air fryer, insert fryer basket, then shut with its lid, set the fryer at 360 degrees F and cook the fritter for 12 minutes until nicely golden and cooked, flipping the fritters halfway through the frying.
7. Serve straight away.

Nutrition Info:
- Calories: 57 CalCarbs: 8 gFat: 1 gProtein: 3 gFiber: 1 g

Salmon Fries

Servings: 4 | Cooking Time: 5 Minutes

Ingredients:
- 1 lb. boneless salmon filets
- 2 cup dry breadcrumbs
- 2 tsp. oregano
- 2 tsp. red chili flakes
- Marinade:
- 1 ½- tbsp. ginger-garlic paste
- 4 tbsp. lemon juice
- 2 tsp. salt
- 1 tsp. pepper powder
- 1 tsp. red chili powder
- 6- tbsp. corn flour
- 4- eggs

Directions:
1. Blend all marinade ingredients and soak the meat for 20-30 minutes.
2. Blend the breadcrumbs, oregano and red chili well and dip the marinated fingers in this mix.
3. Preheat the Air Fryer to 160 F for 5 minutes.
4. Cook for 15 minutes, shaking halfway through.

Nutrition Info:
- Calories: 97 Protein: 1.5g Fiber: 8.0g Fat: 3.3g Carbs: 15.8g

Mini Popovers

Servings: 7 | Cooking Time: 20 Minutes

Ingredients:
- 1 cup milk room temperature
- 2 eggs at room temperature
- 1 tbsp. butter melted
- 1 cup all-purpose flour
- Salt and pepper

Directions:
1. Generously coat a heatproof silicone egg bite mold with non-stick spray.
2. Add all ingredients to a blender and process at medium speed for 30 seconds.
3. Fill each mold with a scant 2 tbsp of batter.
4. Place them into the Instant Pot Duo Crisp Air Fryer Basket.
5. Select the option Air Fryer, Close the Air Fryer lid and cook at 400°F for 20 minutes.
6. After 20 minutes, place the egg bite mold on the lower tray of the Instant Pot Duo Crisp Air Fryer.
7. After it gets cooked, quickly pierce each popover with a sharp knife, then again place them in the Instant Pot Duo Crisp Air Fryer Basket and continue cooking for 2 minutes more.
8. Serve.

Nutrition Info:
- Calories: 135 kcal; Fat: 4.6g; Carbs: 17.9g; Protein: 5.6g

Balsamic Cabbage

Servings: 4 | Cooking Time: Minutes

Ingredients:
- 6 cups red cabbage; shredded
- 4 garlic cloves; minced
- 1 tbsp. olive oil
- 1 tbsp. balsamic vinegar
- Salt and black pepper to taste.

Directions:
1. In a pan that fits the air fryer, combine all the ingredients, toss, introduce the pan in the air fryer and cook at 380°F for 15 minutes
2. Divide between plates and serve as a side dish.

Nutrition Info:
- Calories: 151 Fat: 2g Fiber: 3g Carbs: 5g Protein: 5g

Green Beans

Servings: 4 | Cooking Time: 20 Minutes

Ingredients:
- 6 cups green beans; trimmed
- 1 tbsp. hot paprika
- 2 tbsp. olive oil
- A pinch of salt and black pepper

Directions:
1. Get a bowl and mix the green beans with the other ingredients, toss, put them in the air fryer's basket and cook at 370°F for 20 minutes
2. Divide between plates and serve as a side dish.

Nutrition Info:
- Calories: 120 Fat: 5g Fiber: 1g Carbs: 4g Protein: 2g

Cheesy Bell Pepper Eggs

Servings:4 | Cooking Time: 15 Min

Ingredients:
- 4 medium green bell peppers
- 3 ounces cooked ham, chopped
- 1/4 medium onion, peeled and chopped
- 8 large eggs
- 1 cup mild Cheddar cheese

Directions:
1. Cut each bell pepper from its tops. Pick the seeds with a small knife and the white membranes. Place onion and ham into each pepper.
2. Break two eggs into each chili pepper. Cover with 1/4 cup of peppered cheese. Put the basket into the air fryer.
3. Set the temperature to 390 ° F and change the timer for 15 minutes.
4. Peppers will be tender when fully fried, and the eggs will be solid. Serve hot.

Nutrition Info:
- calories: 314| protein: 24.9g| fiber: 1.7g| net carbohydrates: 4.6g fat: 18.6g| carbohydrates: 6.3g|

Creamy Fennel

Servings: 4 | Cooking Time: 12 Minutes

Ingredients:
- 2 big fennel bulbs; sliced
- ½ cup coconut cream
- 2 tbsp. butter; melted
- Salt and black pepper to taste.

Directions:
1. In a pan that fits the air fryer, combine all the ingredients, toss, introduce in the machine and cook at 370°F for 12 minutes
2. Divide between plates and serve as a side dish.

Nutrition Info:
- Calories: 151 Fat: 3g Fiber: 2g Carbs: 4g Protein: 6g

Spinach And Artichokes Sauté

Servings: 4 | Cooking Time: 15 Minutes

Ingredients:
- 10 oz. artichoke hearts; halved
- 2 cups baby spinach
- 3 garlic cloves
- ¼ cup veggie stock
- 2 tsp. lime juice
- Salt and black pepper to taste.

Directions:
1. In a pan that fits your air fryer, mix all the ingredients, toss, introduce in the fryer and cook at 370°F for 15 minutes
2. Divide between plates and serve as a side dish.

Nutrition Info:
- Calories: 209 Fat: 6g Fiber: 2g Carbs: 4g Protein: 8g

Nutella Smores

Servings: 4 | Cooking Time: 5 Minutes

Ingredients:
- 4 Graham crackers, halved
- 2 half-cut jumbo marshmallows
- Strawberries and Raspberries
- 4 tsps. Nutella

Directions:
1. Preheat the air fryer to 350°F.
2. Place 4 graham cracker halves in the air fryer basket.
3. Put 1 marshmallow on top of each graham cracker half. Cook for 5 minutes, till marshmallow is nice and golden.
4. Add the berries and the Nutella. Top each with a graham cracker half.
5. Serve.

Nutrition Info:
- Calories: 401 kcal; Fat: 15g; Carbs: 61g; Protein: 4g

Fried Garlic Green Tomatoes

Servings: 2 | Cooking Time: 12 Minutes

Ingredients:
- sliced green tomatoes
- 1/2 cup almond flour
- 2 beaten eggs
- Salt and pepper
- 1 tsp. minced garlic

Directions:
1. Season the tomatoes with salt, garlic, and pepper.
2. Preheat your air fryer to 400°F.
3. Dip the tomatoes first in flour then in the egg mixture.
4. Spray the tomato rounds with olive oil and place in the air fryer basket.
5. Cook for 8 minutes, then flip over and cook for an additional 4 minutes. Serve.

Nutrition Info:
- Calories: 123 kcal; Fat: 3.9g; Carbs: 16g; Protein: 8.4g

Avocado Egg Rolls

Servings: 10 | Cooking Time: 15 Minutes

Ingredients:
- Ten egg roll wrappers
- Diced sundried tomatoes: ¼ cup oil drained
- Avocados, cut in cube
- Red onion: 2/3 cup chopped
- 1/3 cup chopped cilantro
- Kosher salt and freshly ground black pepper
- Two small limes: juice

Directions:
1. In a bowl, add sundried tomatoes, avocado, cilantro, lime juice, pepper, onion, and kosher salt mix well gently.
2. Lay egg roll wrapper flat on a surface, add ¼ cup of filling in the wrapper's bottom.
3. Seal with water and make it into a roll.
4. Spray the rolls with olive oil.
5. Cook at 400 F in the air fryer for six minutes. Turn halfway through.
6. Serve with dipping sauce.

Nutrition Info:
- 160 Cal| total fat 19g |carbohydrates 5.6g |protein 19.2g

Air Fried Cheesy Chicken Omelet

Servings: 2 | Cooking Time: 18 Minutes

Ingredients:
- Cooked Chicken Breast: half cup (diced) divided
- Four eggs
- Onion powder: 1/4 tsp, divided
- Salt: 1/2 tsp., divided
- Pepper: 1/4 tsp., divided
- Shredded cheese: 2 tbsp. divided
- Garlic powder: 1/4 tsp, divided

Directions:
1. Take two ramekins, grease with olive oil.
2. Add two eggs to each ramekin. Add cheese with seasoning.
3. Blend to combine. Add 1/4 cup of cooked chicken on top.
4. Cook for 14-18 minutes, in the air fryer at 330 F, or until fully cooked.

Nutrition Info:
- Calories 185 |Proteins 20g |Carbs 10g |Fat 5g |

Air Fryer Buffalo Cauliflower

Servings: 4 | Cooking Time:15 Minutes

Ingredients:
- Homemade buffalo sauce: 1/2 cup
- One head of cauliflower, cut bite-size pieces
- Butter melted: 1 tablespoon
- Olive oil
- Kosher salt & pepper, to taste

Directions:
1. Spray cooking oil on the air fryer basket.
2. In a bowl, add buffalo sauce, melted butter, pepper, and salt. Mix well.
3. Put the cauliflower bits in the air fryer and spray the olive oil over it. Let it cook at 400 F for 7 minutes.
4. Remove the cauliflower from the air fryer and add it to the sauce. Coat the cauliflower well.
5. Put the sauce coated cauliflower back into the air fryer.
6. Cook at 400 F, for 7-8 minutes or until crispy.
7. Take out from the air fryer and serve with dipping sauce.

Nutrition Info:
- Calories 101kcal | Carbohydrates 4g | Protein 3g | Fat: 7g

Air Fryer Roasted Corn

Servings: 4 | Cooking Time: 10 Minutes

Ingredients:
- 4 corn ears
- Olive oil: 2 to 3 teaspoons
- Kosher salt and pepper to taste

Directions:
1. Clean the corn, wash, and pat dry.
2. Fit in the basket of air fryer, cut if need to.
3. Top with olive oil, kosher salt, and pepper.
4. Cook for ten minutes at 400 F.
5. Enjoy crispy roasted corn.

Nutrition Info:
- Kcal 28|Fat 2g|Net carbs 0 g |Protein 7 g

Onion Rings

Servings: 4 | Cooking Time: 32 Minutes

Ingredients:
- 1 large white onion, peeled
- 2/3 cup pork rinds
- 3 tablespoons almond flour
- 1/2 teaspoon garlic powder
- 1/2 teaspoon paprika
- 1/4 teaspoon sea salt
- 3 tablespoons coconut flour
- 2 eggs, pastured

Directions:
1. Switch on the air fryer, insert fryer basket, grease it with olive oil, then shut with its lid, set the fryer at 400 degrees F and preheat for 10 minutes.
2. Meanwhile, slice the peeled onion into ½ inch thick rings.
3. Take a shallow dish, add almond flour and stir in garlic powder, paprika, and pork rinds; take another shallow dish, add coconut flour and salt and stir until mixed.
4. Crack eggs in a bowl and then whisk until combined.
5. Working on one onion ring at a time, first coat onion ring in coconut flour mixture, then it in egg, and coat with pork rind mixture by scooping over the onion until evenly coated.
6. Open the fryer, place coated onion rings in it in a single layer, spray oil over onion rings, close with its lid and cook for 16 minutes until nicely golden and thoroughly cooked, flipping the onion rings halfway through the frying.
7. When air fryer beeps, open its lid, transfer onion rings onto a serving plate and cook the remaining onion rings in the same manner.
8. Serve straight away.

Nutrition Info:
- Calories: 135 CalCarbs: 8 gFat: 7 gProtein: 8 gFiber: 3 g

Roasted Peanut Butter Squash

Servings: 4 | Cooking Time: 22 Minutes

Ingredients:
- 1 butternut squash, peeled
- 1 teaspoon cinnamon
- 1 tablespoon olive oil

Directions:
1. Switch on the air fryer, insert fryer basket, grease it with olive oil, then shut with its lid, set the fryer at 220 degrees F and preheat for 5 minutes.
2. Meanwhile, peel the squash400 cut it into 1-inch pieces, and then place them in a bowl.
3. Drizzle oil over squash pieces, sprinkle with cinnamon and then toss until well coated.
4. Open the fryer, add squash pieces in it, close with its lid and cook for 17 minutes until nicely golden and crispy, shaking every 5 minutes.
5. When air fryer beeps, open its lid, transfer squash onto a serving plate and serve.

Nutrition Info:
- Calories: 116 CalCarbs: 22 gFat: 3 gProtein: 1 gFiber: 4 g

Brussels Sprouts

Servings: 4 | Cooking Time: 30 Minutes

Ingredients:
- 1 lb. Brussels sprouts, halved
- 1 tbsp. melted butter, unsalted
- 1 tbsp. Coconut oil

Directions:
1. Spray coconut oil to the sprouts. Set in the air fryer basket
2. Allow to cook for about 10 minutes at 400°F. Stir halfway.
3. Set from the air fryer and sprinkle with butter.
4. Enjoy.

Nutrition Info:
- Calories: 90 kcal; Protein: 2.9g; Fiber: 3.2g; Fat: 6.1g; Carbs: 7.5g

Air Fryer Egg Rolls

Servings: 3 | Cooking Time: 20 Minutes

Ingredients:
- Coleslaw mix: half bag
- Half onion
- Salt: 1/2 teaspoon
- Half cups of mushrooms
- Lean ground pork: 2 cups
- One stalk of celery
- Wrappers (egg roll)

Directions:
1. Put a skillet over medium flame, add onion and lean ground pork and cook for 5-7 minutes
2. Add coleslaw mixture, salt, mushrooms, and celery to skillet and cook for almost five minutes
3. Lay egg roll wrapper flat and add filling (1/3 cup), roll it up, seal with water.
4. Spray with oil the rolls.
5. Put in the air fryer for 6-8 minutes at 400F, flipping once halfway through.
6. Serve hot.

Nutrition Info:
- Cal 245| Fat: 10g| Net Carbs: 9g|Protein: 11g

Cherry Pies

Servings: 4 | Cooking Time: 10 Minutes

Ingredients:
- 14 oz. pie crusts, refrigerated
- 1/2 cup cherry pie filling
- cooking spray, non-stick
- 3 tbsps. confectioner sugar
- 1/2 tsp. milk

Directions:
1. Spread out the pie crusts. Cut into 6 pies. Place 1-1/2 tbsps, cherry pie filling towards the dough's center.
2. Fold the pie in half and use a fork to press together. Make 3 small cuts to the dough's top. Set in the air fryer.
3. Apply a spraying of the cooking spray at 350°F and cook for 10 minutes.
4. Once done, set aside to cool. Mix the glaze ingredients to get rid of lumps. Sprinkle them over the pies.
5. Enjoy.

Nutrition Info:
- Calories: 270 kcal; Fat: 12g; Carbs: 39g; Proteins: 2.8g

Zucchini Gratin

Servings: 4 | Cooking Time: 15 Minutes

Ingredients:
- Olive oil: 1 tablespoon
- Chopped fresh parsley: 1 tablespoon
- Whole wheat bread crumbs: 2 tablespoons
- Medium zucchini
- Freshly ground black pepper & kosher salt to taste
- Grated Parmesan cheese: 4 tablespoons

Directions:
1. Let the air fryer preheat to 180C.
2. Cut zucchini in half, and a further cut in eight pieces.
3. Place pieces in the air fryer, but do not start frying.
4. In a bowl, add cheese, freshly ground black pepper, parsley, bread crumbs, and oil. Mix well.
5. Add the mixture on top of the zucchini. Then cook the pieces for 15 minutes.
6. Until light golden brown, serve hot and enjoy.

Nutrition Info:
- 81.7 calories| protein 3.6g carbohydrates 6.1g |fat 5.2g

Kale And Walnuts

Servings: 4 | Cooking Time: 15 Minutes

Ingredients:
- 3 garlic cloves
- 10 cups kale; roughly chopped.
- 1/3 cup parmesan; grated
- ½ cup almond milk
- ¼ cup walnuts; chopped.
- 1 tbsp. butter; melted
- ¼ tsp. nutmeg, ground
- Salt and black pepper to taste.

Directions:
1. In a pan that fits the air fryer, combine all the ingredients, toss, introduce the pan in the machine and cook at 360°F for 15 minutes
2. Divide between plates and serve.

Nutrition Info:
- Calories: 160 Fat: 7g Fiber: 2g Carbs: 4g Protein: 5g

Fish Club Sandwich

Servings: 4 | Cooking Time: 15 Minutes

Ingredients:
- 2- slices of white bread
- 1 -tbsp. softened butter
- 1 tin tuna
- 1 small capsicum
- For Barbeque Sauce:
- ¼- tbsp. Worcestershire sauce
- ½- tsp. olive oil
- ½- flake garlic
- ¼- cup chopped onion
- ¼- tsp. mustard powder
- ½- tbsp. sugar
- ¼- tbsp. red chili sauce
- 1 tbsp. tomato ketchup
- ½- cup water.
- A pinch of salt and black pepper

Directions:
1. Cut the bread diagonally.
2. Cook the sauce ingredients and until it thickens.
3. Put the potato to the sauce and mix. Cook the capsicum and strip the skin off. Cut the capsicum into strips. Assemble sandwich filling between bread slices.
4. Preheat the air fryer for 5 minutes at 300 F and cook for 15 minutes.

Nutrition Info:
- Calories 201 Fat 9.1 g Carbohydrates 3.6 g Sugar 0.3 g Protein 26.1 g Cho10sterol 239

Crispy Air Fryer Brussels Sprouts

Servings: 4 | Cooking Time: 10 Minutes

Ingredients:
- Almonds sliced: 1/4 cup
- Brussel sprouts: 2 cups
- Kosher salt
- Parmesan cheese: 1/4 cup grated
- Olive oil: 2 Tablespoons
- Everything bagel seasoning: 2 Tablespoons

Directions:
1. In a saucepan, add Brussel sprouts with two cups of water and let it cook over medium flame for almost ten minutes.
2. Drain the sprouts and cut in half.
3. In a mixing bowl, add sliced brussel sprout with crushed almonds, oil, salt, parmesan cheese, and everything bagel seasoning.
4. Completely coat the sprouts.
5. Cook in the air fryer for 12-15 minutes at 375 F or until light brown.
6. Serve hot.

Nutrition Info:
- Calories: 155kcal | Carbohydrates: 3g | Protein: 6g | Fat: 3g |

Herbed Radish Sauté

Servings: 4 | Cooking Time: 15 Minutes

Ingredients:
- 2 bunches red radishes; halved
- 2 tbsp. parsley; chopped.
- 2 tbsp. balsamic vinegar
- 1 tbsp. olive oil
- Salt and black pepper to taste

Directions:
1. Get a bowl and mix the radishes with the remaining ingredients except the parsley, toss and put them in your air fryer's basket.
2. Cook at 400°F for 15 minutes, divide between plates, sprinkle the parsley on top and serve as a side dish.

Nutrition Info:
- Calories: 180 Fat: 4g Fiber: 2g Carbs: 3g Protein: 5g

Poultry Recipes

Poultry Recipes

Lemon Pepper Chicken Breast

Servings: 2 | Cooking Time:15 Minutes

Ingredients:
- Two Lemons rind, juice, and zest
- One Chicken Breast
- Minced Garlic: 1 Tsp
- Black Peppercorns: 2 tbsp.
- Chicken Seasoning: 1 Tbsp.
- Salt & pepper, to taste

Directions:
1. Let the air fryer preheat to 180C.
2. In a large aluminum foil, add all the seasonings along with lemon rind.
3. Add salt and pepper to chicken and rub the seasonings all over chicken breast.
4. Put the chicken in aluminum foil. And fold it tightly.
5. Flatten the chicken inside foil with a rolling pin
6. Put it in the air fryer and cook at 180 C for 15 minutes.
7. Serve hot.

Nutrition Info:
- Calories: 140 | Carbohydrates: 24g | Protein: 13g | Fat: 2g

Buttermilk Chicken In Air-fryer

Servings: 6 | Cooking Time:20 Minutes

Ingredients:
- Chicken thighs: 4 cups skin-on, bone-in
- Marinade
- Buttermilk: 2 cups
- Black pepper: 2 tsp.
- Cayenne pepper: 1 tsp.
- Salt: 2 tsp.
- Seasoned Flour
- Baking powder: 1 tbsp.
- All-purpose flour: 2 cups
- Paprika powder: 1 tbsp.
- Salt: 1 tsp.
- Garlic powder: 1 tbsp.

Directions:
1. Let the air fry heat at 180 C.
2. With a paper towel, pat dry the chicken thighs.
3. In a mixing bowl, add paprika, black pepper, salt mix well, then add chicken pieces. Add buttermilk and coat the chicken well. Let it marinate for at least 6 hours.
4. In another bowl, add baking powder, salt, flour, pepper, and paprika. Put one by one of the chicken pieces and coat in the seasoning mix.
5. Spray oil on chicken pieces and place breaded chicken skin side up in air fryer basket in one layer, cook for 8 minutes, then flip the chicken pieces' cook for another ten minutes
6. Take out from the air fryer and serve right away.

Nutrition Info:
- Cal 210|fat 18 g| protein 22g|carbs 12 g

Breaded Chicken With Seed Chips

Servings: 4 | Cooking Time: 40 Minutes

Ingredients:
- 12 chicken breast fillets
- Salt
- 2 eggs
- 1 small bag of seed chips
- Breadcrumbs
- Extra virgin olive oil

Directions:
1. Put salt to chicken fillets.
2. Crush the seed chips and when we have them fine, bind with the breadcrumbs.
3. Beat the two eggs.
4. Pass the chicken breast fillets through the beaten egg and then through the seed chips that you have tied with the breadcrumbs.
5. When you have them all breaded, paint with a brush of extra virgin olive oil.
6. Place the fillets in the basket of the air fryer without being piled up.
7. Select 170 degrees, 20 minutes.
8. Take out and put another batch, repeat temperature and time. So, until you use up all the steaks.

Nutrition Info:
- Calories: 242 Fat: 13g Carbohydrates: 13.5g Protein: 18g Sugar: 0g Cholesterol: 42mg

Crispy Chicken Thighs

Servings: 2 | Cooking Time: 20 Minutes

Ingredients:
- chicken thighs, skin on, bone removed, pat dry
- salt
- garlic powder
- black pepper

Directions:
1. Preheat the Air Fryer to 4000F. Season the chicken with salt and pepper. Place the chicken in the Air Fryer basket.
2. Cook at 4000F for 18 minutes and top with black pepper.
3. Serve.

Nutrition Info:
- Calories: 104 kcal; Protein: 13.5g; Carbs: 0g; Fat: 5.7g

Jerk Style Chicken Wings

Servings: 2-3 | Cooking Time: 25 Minutes

Ingredients:
- 1g ground thyme
- 1g dried rosemary
- 2g allspice
- 4g ground ginger
- 3 g garlic powder
- 2g onion powder
- 1g of cinnamon
- 2g of paprika
- 2g chili powder
- 1g nutmeg
- Salt to taste
- 30 ml of vegetable oil
- 0.5 - 1 kg of chicken wings
- 1 lime, juice

Directions:
1. Select Preheat, set the temperature to 200°C and press Start/Pause.
2. Combine all spices and oil in a bowl to create a marinade.
3. Mix the chicken wings in the marinade until they are well covered.
4. Place the chicken wings in the preheated air fryer.
5. Select Chicken and press Start/Pause. Be sure to shake the baskets in the middle of cooking.
6. Remove the wings and place them on a serving plate.
7. Squeeze fresh lemon juice over the wings and serve.

Nutrition Info:
- Calories: 240 Fat: 15gCarbohydrate: 5g Protein: 19g Sugars: 4g Cholesterol: 60mg

Air Fried Blackened Chicken Breast

Servings: 2 | Cooking Time: 20 Minutes

Ingredients:
- Paprika: 2 teaspoons
- Ground thyme: 1 teaspoon
- Cumin: 1 teaspoon
- Cayenne pepper: half tsp.
- Onion powder: half tsp.
- Black Pepper: half tsp.
- Salt: ¼ teaspoon
- Vegetable oil: 2 teaspoons
- Pieces of chicken breast halves (without bones and skin)

Directions:
1. In a mixing bowl, add onion powder, salt, cumin, paprika, black pepper, thyme, and cayenne pepper. Mix it well.
2. Drizzle oil over chicken and rub. Dip each piece of chicken in blackening spice blend on both sides.
3. Let it rest for five minutes while the air fryer is preheating.
4. Preheat it for five minutes at 360F.
5. Put the chicken in the air fryer and let it cook for ten minutes. Flip and then cook for another ten minutes.
6. After, let it sit for five minutes, then slice and serve with the side of greens.

Nutrition Info:
- 432.1 calories| protein 79.4g| carbohydrates 3.2g| fat 9.5g

Crispy Ranch Air Fryer Nuggets

Servings: 2 | Cooking Time: 25 Minutes

Ingredients:
- 1 lb. poultry tenders, sliced into 2-inch pieces
- 1 oz. bundle completely dry cattle ranch salad dressing mix.
- 2 tbsps. flour
- 1 gently beaten egg
- 1 cup panko bread crumbs

Directions:
1. Arrange poultry in a dish, spray with ranch seasoning, as well as toss to integrate. Allow to sit for 10 minutes.
2. Place flour in a resealable bag. Place egg in a little bowl as well as panko bread crumbs on a plate. Adjust the temperature of the air fryer to 391°F.
3. Set poultry into the bag and also toss to layer. Gently dip chicken into egg combination, letting excess drip off. Roll poultry items in panko, pressing crumbs right into the poultry.
4. Spray basket of the air fryer with oil and place chicken items within, making sure not to overlap. You might have to do three batches, depending on the dimension of your air fryer. Gently haze chicken with cooking spray.
5. Cook for 4 minutes. Transform chicken items and also cook until the chicken is not pinker on the inside. Serve.

Nutrition Info:
- Calories:244 kcal; Carbs: 25.3g; Protein: 31g; Fat:3.6 g

Orange Chicken Wings

Servings: 2 | Cooking Time: 14 Minutes

Ingredients:
- Honey: 1 tbsp.
- Chicken Wings, Six pieces
- One orange zest and juice
- Worcestershire Sauce: 1.5 tbsp.
- Black pepper to taste
- Herbs (sage, rosemary, oregano, parsley, basil, thyme, and mint)

Directions:
1. Wash and pat dry the chicken wings
2. In a bowl, add chicken wings, pour zest and orange juice
3. Add the rest of the ingredients and rub on chicken wings. Let it marinate for at least half an hour.
4. Let the Air fryer preheat at 180°C
5. In an aluminum foil, wrap the marinated wings and put them in an air fryer, and cook for 20 minutes at 180 C
6. After 20 minutes, remove aluminum foil and brush the sauce over wings and cook for 15 minutes more. Then again, brush the sauce and cook for another ten minutes.
7. Take out from the air fryer and serve hot.

Nutrition Info:
- Calories 271 |Proteins 29g |Carbs 20g |Fat 15g |

Southwest Chicken In Air Fryer

Servings: 4 | Cooking Time:30 Minutes

Ingredients:
- Avocado oil: one tbsp.
- Four cups of boneless, skinless, chicken breast
- Chili powder: half tsp.
- Salt to taste
- Cumin: half tsp.
- Onion powder: 1/4 tsp.
- Lime juice: two tbsp.
- Garlic powder: 1/4 tsp

Directions:
1. In a ziploc bag, add chicken, oil, and lime juice.
2. Add all spices in a bowl and rub all over the chicken in the ziploc bag.
3. Let it marinate in the fridge for ten minutes or more.
4. Take chicken out from the ziploc bag and put it in the air fryer.
5. Cook for 25 minutes at 400 F, flipping chicken halfway through until internal temperature reaches 165 degrees.

Nutrition Info:
- Calories: 165kcal|Carbohydrates: 1g|Protein: 24g|Fat: 6g

Air Fried Maple Chicken Thighs

Servings: 4 | Cooking Time: 25 minutes

Ingredients:
- One egg
- Buttermilk: 1 cup
- Maple syrup: half cup
- Chicken thighs: 4 pieces
- Granulated garlic: 1 tsp.
- Dry Mix
- Granulated garlic: half tsp.
- All-purpose flour: half cup
- Salt: one tbsp.
- Sweet paprika: one tsp.
- Smoked paprika: half tsp.
- Tapioca flour: ¼ cup
- Cayenne pepper: ¼ teaspoon
- Granulated onion: one tsp.
- Black pepper: ¼ teaspoon
- Honey powder: half tsp.

Directions:
1. In a ziploc bag, add egg, one tsp. of granulated garlic, buttermilk, and maple syrup, add in the chicken thighs and let it marinate for one hour or more in the refrigerator
2. In a mixing bowl, add sweet paprika, tapioca flour, granulated onion, half tsp. of granulated garlic, flour, cayenne pepper, salt, pepper, honey powder, and smoked paprika mix it well.
3. Let the air fry preheat to 380 F
4. Coat the marinated chicken thighs in the dry spice mix, shake the excess off.
5. Put the chicken skin side down in the air fryer
6. Let it cook for 12 minutes. Flip thighs halfway through and cook for 13 minutes more.
7. Serve with salad greens.

Nutrition Info:
- 415.4 calories| protein 23.3g| carbohydrates 20.8g| fat 13.4g

Chicken Wings

Servings: 4 | Cooking Time: 1 Hour And 30 Minutes

Ingredients:
- 3 pounds chicken wing parts, pastured
- 1 tablespoon old bay seasoning
- 1 teaspoon lemon zest
- 3/4 cup potato starch
- 1/2 cup butter, unsalted, melted

Directions:
1. Switch on the air fryer, insert fryer basket, grease it with olive oil, then shut with its lid, set the fryer at 360 degrees F and preheat for 5 minutes.
2. Meanwhile, pat dry chicken wings and then place them in a bowl.
3. Stir together seasoning and starch, add to chicken wings and stir well until evenly coated.
4. Open the fryer, add chicken wings in it in a single layer, close with its lid and cook for 35 minutes, shaking every 10 minutes.
5. Then switch the temperature of air fryer to 400 degrees F and continue air frying the chicken wings for 10 minutes or until nicely golden brown and cooked, shaking every 3 minutes.
6. When air fryer beeps, open its lid, transfer chicken wings onto a serving plate and cook the remaining wings in the same manner.
7. Whisk together melted butter and lemon zest until blended and serve it with the chicken wings.

Nutrition Info:
- Calories: 240 CalCarbs: 4 gFat: 16 gProtein: 20 gFiber: 0 g

Buttermilk Fried Chicken

Servings: 4 | Cooking Time: 10 Minutes

Ingredients:
- 3 tablespoons cornmeal, ground
- 1-pound chicken breasts, pastured
- 6 tablespoons cornflakes
- 1 teaspoon garlic powder
- ¼ teaspoon ground black pepper
- 1 teaspoon paprika
- ¼ teaspoon salt
- ¼ teaspoon hot sauce
- 1/3 cup buttermilk, low-fat

Directions:
1. Pour milk in a bowl, add hot sauce and whisk until well mixed.
2. Cut the chicken in half lengthwise into four pieces, then add into buttermilk, toss well until well coated and let it sit for 15 minutes.
3. Place cornflakes in a blender or food processor, pulse until mixture resembles crumbs, then add remaining ingredients, pulse until well mixed and then tip the mixture into a shallow dish.
4. After 15 minutes, remove chicken from the buttermilk, then coat with cornflakes mixture until evenly coated and place the chicken on a wire rack.
5. Switch on the air fryer, insert fryer basket, grease it with olive oil, then shut with its lid, set the fryer at 375 degrees F and preheat for 5 minutes.
6. Then open the fryer, add chicken in it in a single layer, spray with oil, close with its lid and cook for 10 minutes until nicely golden and cooked, turning the chicken halfway through the frying.
7. When air fryer beeps, open its lid, transfer chicken onto a serving plate and serve.

Nutrition Info:
- Calories: 160 CalCarbs: 7 gFat: 3.5 gProtein: 24 gFiber: 1 g

Mushroom Oatmeal

Servings: 4 | Cooking Time: 20 Min

Ingredients:
- One small yellow onion, chopped
- 1 cup steel-cut oats
- 1 Garlic cloves, minced
- 2 Tablespoons butter
- ½ cup of water
- One and a half cup of canned chicken stock
- Thyme springs, chopped
- 2 Tablespoons extra virgin olive oil
- ½ cup gouda cheese, grated
- 1 cup mushroom, sliced
- Salt and black pepper to taste

Directions:
1. Heat a pan over medium heat, which suits your air fryer with the butter, add onions and garlic, stir and cook for 4 minutes.
2. Add oats, sugar, salt, pepper, stock, and thyme, stir, place in the air fryer and cook for 16 minutes at 360 degrees F.
3. In the meantime, prepare a skillet over medium heat with the olive oil, add mushrooms, cook them for 3 minutes, add oatmeal and cheese, whisk, divide into bowls and serve for breakfast.
4. Enjoy.

Nutrition Info:
- calories 284|fat 8g| fiber 8g|carbs 20g| protein 17g

Air Fryer Chicken Cheese Quesadilla

Servings: 3 | Cooking Time: 6 Minutes

Ingredients:
- 2 flour tortillas.
- 1 cup precooked hen diced.
- 1 mug shredded cheese.

Directions:
1. Set one flour tortilla into the air fryer. Add in cheese and chicken. Spread equally.
2. Top with the second tortilla. Place a metal shelf on the top to keep it from moving.
3. Prepare at 370F for 6 mins, flipping half means.
4. Cut and also serve.

Nutrition Info:
- Calories: 171 kcal; Carbs: 8 g; Protein: 15g; Fat: 8 g.

Garlic-roasted Chicken With Creamer Potatoes

Servings:4 | Cooking Time:x

Ingredients:
- 1 (2½-to 3-pound) broiler-fryer whole chicken
- 2 tablespoons olive oil
- ½-teaspoon garlic salt
- 8 cloves garlic, peeled
- 1 slice lemon
- ½ teaspoon dried thyme
- ½ teaspoon dried marjoram
- 12 to 16 creamer potatoes, scrubbed

Directions:
1. Do not wash the chicken before cooking. Remove it from its packaging and pat the chicken dry.
2. Combine the olive oil and salt in a small bowl. Rub half of this mixture on the inside of the chicken, under the skin, and on the chicken skin. Place the garlic cloves and lemon slice inside the chicken. Sprinkle the chicken with the thyme and marjoram
3. Put the chicken in the air fryer basket. Surround with the potatoes and drizzle the potatoes with the remaining olive oil mixture.
4. Roast for 25 minutes, and then test the temperature of the chicken. It should be 160°F. Test at the thickest part of the breast, making sure the probe does not touch bone. If the chicken is not done yet, return it to the air fryer and roast it for 4 to 5 minutes, or until the temperature is 160°F.
5. When the chicken is done, transfer it and the potatoes to a serving platter and cover with foil. Let the chicken rest for 5 minutes before serving.

Nutrition Info:
- Calories: 491 Fat: 13g Carbohydrates: 1g Protein: 2Sugar: 1gCholesterol: 170mg

Chicken Cheesey Quesadilla In Air Fryer

Servings: 4 | Cooking Time: 7 Minutes

Ingredients:
- Precooked chicken: one cup, diced
- Tortillas: 2 pieces
- Low-fat cheese: one cup (shredded)

Directions:
1. Spray oil the air basket and place one tortilla in it. Add cooked chicken and cheese on top.
2. Add the second tortilla on top. Put a metal rack on top.
3. Cook for 6 minutes at 370 degrees, flip it halfway through so cooking evenly.
4. Slice and serve with dipping sauce.

Nutrition Info:
- Calories: 171kcal | Carbohydrates: 8g | Protein: 15g | Fat: 8g |

Fried Lemon Chicken

Servings: Six | Cooking Time: 20 Minutes

Ingredients:
- 6 chicken thighs
- 2 tbsp. olive oil
- 2 tbsp. lemon juice
- 1 tbsp. Italian herbal seasoning mix
- 1 tsp. Celtic sea salt
- 1 tsp. ground fresh pepper
- 1 lemon, thinly slice

Directions:
1. Add all ingredients, except sliced lemon, to bowl or bag, stir to cover chicken.
2. Let marinate for 30 minutes overnight.
3. Remove the chicken and let the excess oil drip (it does not need to dry out, just do not drip with tons of excess oil).
4. Arrange the chicken thighs and the lemon slices in the fryer basket, being careful not to push the chicken thighs too close to each other.
5. Set the fryer to 200 degrees and cook for 10 minutes.
6. Remove the basket from the fryer and turn the chicken thighs to the other side.
7. Cook again at 200 for another 10 minutes.

Nutrition Info:
- Calories: 215 Fat: 13g Carbohydrates: 1g Protein: 2Sugar: 1gCholesterol: 130mg

Air Fryer Pork Chop & Broccoli

Servings: 2 | Cooking Time:20 Minutes

Ingredients:
- Broccoli florets: 2 cups
- Bone-in pork chop: 2 pieces
- Paprika: half tsp.
- Avocado oil: 2 tbsp.
- Garlic powder: half tsp.
- Onion powder: half tsp.
- Two cloves of crushed garlic
- Salt: 1 teaspoon divided

Directions:
1. Let the air fryer preheat to 350 degrees. Spray the basket with cooking oil
2. Add one tbsp. Oil, onion powder, half tsp. of salt, garlic powder, and paprika in a bowl mix well, rub this spice mix to the pork chop's sides
3. Add pork chops to air fryer basket and let it cook for five minutes
4. In the meantime, add one tsp. oil, garlic, half tsp of salt, and broccoli to a bowl and coat well
5. Flip the pork chop and add the broccoli, let it cook for five more minutes.
6. Take out from the air fryer and serve.

Nutrition Info:
- Calories 483|Total Fat 20g|Carbohydrates 12g|protein 23 g

Ham And Cheese Stuffed Chicken Burgers

Servings:4 | Cooking Time:x

Ingredients:
- ⅓ Cup soft bread crumbs
- 3 tablespoons milk
- 1 egg, beaten
- ½ teaspoon dried thyme
- Pinch salt
- Freshly ground black pepper
- 1¼ pounds ground chicken
- ¼ cup finely chopped ham
- ⅓ cup grated Havarti cheese
- Olive oil for misting

Directions:
1. In a medium bowl, combine the breadcrumbs, milk, egg, thyme, salt, and pepper. Add the chicken and mix gently but thoroughly with clean hands.
2. Form the chicken into eight thin patties and place on waxed paper.
3. Top four of the patties with the ham and cheese. Top with remaining four patties and gently press the edges together to seal, so the ham and cheese mixture is in the middle of the burger.
4. Place the burgers in the basket and mist with olive oil. Grill for 13 to 16 minutes or until the chicken is thoroughly cooked to 165°F as measured with a meat thermometer.

Nutrition Info:
- Calories: 324 Fat: 13g Carbohydrates: 1g Protein: 2Sugar: 1gCholesterol: 130mg

Lemon Chicken With Basil

Servings: 4 | Cooking Time: 1h

Ingredients:
- 1kg chopped chicken
- 2 lemons
- Basil, salt and ground pepper
- Extra virgin olive oil

Directions:
1. Put the chicken in a bowl with a jet of extra virgin olive oil.
2. Put salt, pepper, and basil.
3. Bind well and let stand for at least 30 minutes, stirring occasionally.
4. Put the pieces of chicken in the air fryer basket and take the air fryer
5. Select 30 minutes.
6. Occasionally remove.
7. Take out and put another batch.
8. Repeat the same process.

Nutrition Info:
- Calories: 1,440 kcal; Fat: 74.9g; Carbs: 122.0g; Protein: 68.6g

Buffalo Chicken Hot Wings

Servings: 6 | Cooking Time: 45 Minutes

Ingredients:
- 16 chicken wings, pastured
- 1 teaspoon garlic powder
- 2 teaspoons chicken seasoning
- ¾ teaspoon ground black pepper
- 2 teaspoons soy sauce
- 1/4 cup buffalo sauce, reduced-fat

Directions:
1. Switch on the air fryer, insert fryer basket, grease it with olive oil, then shut with its lid, set the fryer at 400 degrees F and preheat for 5 minutes.
2. Meanwhile, place chicken wings in a bowl, drizzle with soy sauce, toss until well coated and then season with black pepper and garlic powder.
3. Open the fryer, stack chicken wings in it, then spray with oil and close with its lid.
4. Cook the chicken wings for 10 minutes, turning the wings halfway through, and then transfer them to a bowl, covering the bowl with a foil to keep the chicken wings warm.
5. Air fry the remaining chicken wings in the same manner, then transfer them to the bowl, add buffalo sauce and toss until well coated.
6. Return chicken wings into the fryer basket in a single layer and continue frying for 7 to 12 minutes or until chicken wings are glazed and crispy, shaking the chicken wings every 3 to 4 minutes.
7. Serve straight away.

Nutrition Info:
- Calories: 88 CalCarbs: 2.6 gFat: 6.5 gProtein: 4.5 gFiber: 0.1 g

Lemon Rosemary Chicken

Servings: 2 | Cooking Time:20 Minutes

Ingredients:
- For marinade
- Chicken: 2 and ½ cups
- Ginger: 1 tsp, minced
- Olive oil: 1/2 tbsp.
- Soy sauce: 1 tbsp.
- For the sauce
- Half lemon
- Honey: 3 tbsp.
- Oyster sauce: 1 tbsp.
- Fresh rosemary: half cup, chopped

Directions:
1. In a big mixing bowl, add the marinade ingredients with chicken, and mix well.
2. Keep in the refrigerator for at least half an hour.
3. Let the oven preheat to 200 C for three minutes.
4. Place the marinated chicken in the air fryer in a single layer. And cook for 6 minutes at 200 degrees.
5. Meanwhile, add all the sauces ingredients in a bowl and mix well except for lemon wedges.
6. Brush the sauce generously over half-baked chicken add lemon juice on top.
7. Cook for another 13 minutes at 200 C. flip the chicken halfway through. Let the chicken evenly brown.
8. Serve right away and enjoy.

Nutrition Info:
- Calories 308 |Proteins 25g |Carbs 7g|Fat 12 g |

Garlic Parmesan Chicken Tenders

Servings: 4 | Cooking Time:12 Minutes

Ingredients:
- One egg
- Eight raw chicken tenders
- Water: 2 tablespoons
- Olive oil
- To coat
- Panko breadcrumbs: 1 cup
- Half tsp of salt
- Black Pepper: 1/4 teaspoon
- Garlic powder: 1 teaspoon
- Onion powder: 1/2 teaspoon
- Parmesan cheese: 1/4 cup
- Any dipping Sauce

Directions:
1. Add all the coating ingredients in a big bowl
2. In another bowl, mix water and egg.
3. Dip the chicken in the egg mix, then in the coating mix.
4. Put the tenders in the air fry basket in a single layer.
5. Spray with the olive oil light
6. Cook at 400 degrees for 12 minutes. Flip the chicken halfway through.
7. Serve with salad greens and enjoy.

Nutrition Info:
- Calories: 220 | Carbohydrates: 13g | Protein: 27g | Fat: 6g |

Pork Rind Nachos

Servings:2 | Cooking Time: 5 Min

Ingredients:
- 2 tbsp. of pork rinds
- 1/4 cup shredded cooked chicken
- 1/2 cup shredded Monterey jack cheese
- 1/4 cup sliced pickled jalapeños
- 1/4 cup guacamole
- 1/4 cup full-fat sour cream

Directions:
1. Put pork rinds in a 6 "round baking pan. Fill with grilled chicken and Monterey cheese jack. Place the pan in the basket with the air fryer.
2. Set the temperature to 370 ° F and set the timer for 5 minutes or until the cheese has been melted.
3. Eat right away with jalapeños, guacamole, and sour cream.

Nutrition Info:
- calories 295 |protein: 30.1 g| fiber: 1.2 g| net carbohydrates: 1.8 g |fat: 27.5 g| carbohydrates: 3.0 g |

Breaded Chicken Tenderloins

Servings: 4 | Cooking Time:12 Minutes

Ingredients:
- Eight chicken tenderloins
- Olive oil: 2 tablespoons
- One egg whisked
- 1/4 cup breadcrumbs

Directions:
1. Let the air fryer heat to 180 C.
2. In a big bowl, add breadcrumbs and oil, mix well until forms a crumbly mixture
3. Dip chicken tenderloin in whisked egg and coat in breadcrumbs mixture.
4. Place the breaded chicken in the air fryer and cook at 180C for 12 minutes or more.
5. Take out from the air fryer and serve with your favorite green salad.

Nutrition Info:
- Calories 206|Proteins 20g |Carbs 17g |Fat 10g |

Chicken Skewers With Yogurt

Servings: 2-4 | Cooking Time: 10 Minutes

Ingredients:
- 123g of plain whole milk Greek yogurt
- 20 ml of olive oil
- 2g of paprika
- 1g cumin
- 1g crushed red pepper
- 1 lemon, juice and zest of the peel
- 5g of salt
- 1g freshly ground black pepper
- 4 cloves garlic, minced
- 454g chicken thighs, boneless, skinless, cut into 38 mm pieces
- 2 wooden skewers, cut in half
- Nonstick Spray Oil

Directions:
1. Mix the yogurt, olive oil, paprika, cumin, red paprika, lemon juice, lemon zest, salt, pepper, and garlic in a large bowl.
2. Add the chicken to the marinade and marinate in the fridge for at least 4 hours.
3. Select Preheat and press Start/Pause.
4. Cut the marinated chicken thighs into 38 mm pieces and spread them on skewers.
5. Place the skewers in the preheated air fryer.
6. Cook at 200°C for 10 minutes.

Nutrition Info:
- Calories: 113 Fat: 3.4 Carbohydrates: 0g Protein: 20.6g

Tasty Chicken Tenders

Servings: 4 | Cooking Time: 25 Minutes

Ingredients:
- 1 ½ lbs chicken tenders
- 1 tbsp. extra virgin olive oil
- 1 tsp. rotisserie chicken seasoning
- 2 tbsp. BBQ sauce

Directions:
1. Add all ingredients except oil in a zip-lock bag.
2. Seal bag and place in the refrigerator for 2-3 hours.
3. Heat oil in a large pan over medium heat.
4. Cook marinated chicken tenders in a pan until lightly brown and cooked.

Nutrition Info:
- Calories 365 Fat 16.1 g, Carbohydrates 2.8 g, Sugar 2 g, Protein 49.2 g, Cholesterol 151 mg

Chicken Sandwich

Servings: 6 | Cooking Time: 20 Minutes

Ingredients:
- 4 chicken breasts, pastured
- 1 cup almond flour
- ¾ teaspoon ground black pepper
- 1/2 teaspoon paprika
- 1 teaspoon salt
- 1/2 teaspoon celery seeds
- 1 teaspoon potato starch
- 1/4 cup milk, reduced-fat
- 4 cups dill pickle juice as needed
- 2 eggs, pastured
- 4 hamburger buns
- 1/8 teaspoon dry milk powder, nonfat
- ¼ teaspoon xanthan gum
- 1/8 teaspoon erythritol sweetener

Directions:
1. Place the chicken in a large plastic bag, seal the bag and then pound the chicken with a mallet until ½-inch thick.
2. Brine the chicken and for this, pour the dill pickle juice in the plastic bag containing chicken, then seal it and let the chicken soak for a minimum of 2 hours.
3. After 2 hours, remove the chicken from the brine, rinse it well, and pat dry with paper towels.
4. Place flour in a shallow dish, add black pepper, paprika, salt, celery, potato starch, milk powder, xanthan gum, and sweetener and stir until well mixed.
5. Crack eggs in another dish and then whisk until blended.
6. Switch on the air fryer, insert fryer basket, grease it with olive oil, then shut with its lid, set the fryer at 375 degrees F and preheat for 5 minutes.
7. Meanwhile, dip the chicken into the egg and then coat evenly with the flour mixture.
8. Open the fryer, add chicken breasts in it in a single layer, close with its lid, then cook for 10 minutes, flip the chickens and continue cooking for 5 minutes or until chicken is nicely golden and cooked.
9. When air fryer beeps, open its lid, transfer chicken into a plate and cook remaining chicken in the same manner.
10. Sandwich a chicken breast between toasted hamburger buns, top with favorite dressing and serve.

Nutrition Info:
- Calories: 440 CalCarbs: 40 gFat: 19 gProtein: 28 gFiber: 12 g

Jamaican Jerk Pork In Air Fryer

Servings: 4 | Cooking Time:20 Minutes

Ingredients:
- Pork, cut into three-inch pieces
- Jerk paste: ¼ cup

Directions:
1. Rub jerk paste all over the pork pieces.
2. Let it marinate for four hours, at least, in the refrigerator. Or for more time.
3. Let the air fryer preheat to 390 F. spray with olive oil
4. Before putting in the air fryer, let the meat sit for 20 minutes at room temperature.
5. Cook for 20 minutes at 390 F in the air fryer, flip halfway through.
6. Take out from the air fryer let it rest for ten minutes before slicing.
7. Serve with microgreens.

Nutrition Info:
- Calories: 234kcal | Protein: 31g | Fat: 9g |carbs 12 g

Popcorn Chicken In Air Fryer

Servings: 4 | Cooking Time:20 Minutes

Ingredients:
- For Marinade
- 8 cups, chicken tenders, cut into bite-size pieces
- Freshly ground black pepper: 1/2 tsp
- Almond milk: 2 cups
- Salt: 1 tsp
- paprika: 1/2 tsp
- Dry Mix
- Salt: 3 tsp
- Flour: 3 cups
- Paprika: 2 tsp
- Oil spray
- Freshly ground black pepper: 2 tsp

Directions:
1. In a bowl, add all marinade ingredients and chicken. Mix well, and put it in a ziploc bag and refrigerator for two hours for the minimum, or six hours.
2. In a large bowl, add all the dry ingredients.
3. Coat the marinated chicken to the dry mix. Into the marinade again, then for the second time in the dry mixture.
4. Spray the air fryer basket with olive oil and place the breaded chicken pieces in one single layer. Spray oil over the chicken pieces too.
5. Cook at 370 degrees for 10 minutes, tossing halfway through.
6. Serve immediately with salad greens or dipping sauce.

Nutrition Info:
- Calories 340 |Proteins 20g |Carbs 14g |Fat 10g |

Beef, Pork And Lamb Recipes

Beef, Pork And Lamb Recipes

Herbed Lamb Chops

Servings: 6 | Cooking Time: 13 Minutes

Ingredients:
- 1-pound lamb chops, pastured
- For the Marinate:
- 2 tablespoons lemon juice
- 1 teaspoon dried rosemary
- 1 teaspoon salt
- 1 teaspoon dried thyme
- 1 teaspoon coriander
- 1 teaspoon dried oregano
- 2 tablespoons olive oil

Directions:
1. Prepare the marinade and for this, place all its ingredients in a bowl and whisk until combined.
2. Pour the marinade in a large plastic bag, add lamb chops in it, seal the bag, then turn it upside down to coat lamb chops with the marinade and let it marinate in the refrigerator for a minimum of 1 hour.
3. Then switch on the air fryer, insert fryer basket, grease it with olive oil, then shut with its lid, set the fryer at 390 degrees F and preheat for 5 minutes.
4. Meanwhile,
5. Open the fryer, add marinated lamb chops in it, close with its lid and cook for 8 minutes until nicely golden and cooked, turning the lamb chops halfway through the frying.
6. When air fryer beeps, open its lid, transfer lamb chops onto a serving plate and serve.

Nutrition Info:
- Calories: 177.4 CalCarbs: 1.7 gFat: 8 gProtein: 23.4 gFiber: 0.5 g

Fish And Vegetable Tacos

Servings: 4 | Cooking Time: 9 To 12 Minutes

Ingredients:
- 1 pound white fish fillets, such as sole or cod
- 2 teaspoons olive oil
- 3 tablespoons freshly squeezed lemon juice, divided
- 1½ cups chopped red cabbage
- 1 large carrot, grated
- ½ cup low-sodium salsa
- ⅓ cup low-fat Greek yogurt
- 4 soft low-sodium whole-wheat tortillas

Directions:
1. Scrub the fish with the olive oil and drizzle with 1 tablespoon of lemon juice. Fry in the air fryer basket for 9 to 12 minutes, or till the fish just flakes when tested with a fork.
2. For the meantime, in a medium bowl, stir together the remaining 2 tablespoons of lemon juice, the red cabbage, carrot, salsa, and yogurt.
3. Once the fish is cooked, remove it from the air fryer basket and break it up into large pieces.

Nutrition Info:
- Calories: 209 Fat: 3g (13% of calories from fat) Saturated Fat: 0g Protein: 18g Carbohydrates: 30g Sodium: 116mg Fiber: 1g Sugar: 4g 70% DV vitamin A 43% DV vitamin C

Short Ribs

Servings: 6 | Cooking Time: 6 Hours

Ingredients:
- 4 lbs. lean beef short ribs
- 1 tablespoon canola oil
- ¼ cup onion, chopped
- ½ cup celery, chopped
- 3 garlic cloves, minced
- 8 oz. can tomato sauce
- ¼ teaspoon paprika
- ½ teaspoon black pepper

Directions:
1. Heat oil in a skillet over high heat. Add ribs, cook and brown all sides. Add ribs to a slow cooker.
2. Mix the remaining ingredients in a bowl and add over the ribs. Cover and cook for 6 hours on high heat. Serve

Nutrition Info:
- Calories: 769 Fat: 3.41g Carbohydrates: 0g Protein: 20.99g Sugar: 0g

Warm Chicken And Spinach Salad

Servings: 4 | Cooking Time: 16 To 20 Minutes

Ingredients:
- 3 (5-ounce) low-sodium boneless skinless chicken breasts, cut into 1-inch cubes
- 5 teaspoons olive oil
- ½ teaspoon dried thyme
- 1 medium red onion, sliced
- 1 red bell pepper, sliced
- 1 small zucchini, cut into strips
- 3 tablespoons freshly squeezed lemon juice
- 6 cups fresh baby spinach

Directions:
1. In a large bowl, mix the chicken with the olive oil and thyme. Toss to coat. Transfer to a medium metal bowl and roast for 8 minutes in the air fryer.
2. Add the red onion, red bell pepper, and zucchini. Roast for 8 to 12 minutes more, stirring once during cooking, or until the chicken reaches an internal temperature of 165°F on a meat thermometer.
3. Remove the bowl from the air fryer and stir in the lemon juice.
4. Put the spinach in a serving bowl and top with the chicken mixture. Toss to combine and serve immediately.

Nutrition Info:
- Calories: 214 Fat: 7g (29% of calories from fat) Saturated Fat: 1g Protein: 28g Carbohydrates: 7g Sodium: 116mg Fiber: 2g Sugar: 4g 90% DV vitamin A 69% DV vitamin C

Cinnamon Spiced Popcorn

Servings: 4 | Cooking Time: 5 Minutes

Ingredients:
- 8 cups air-popped corn
- 2 teaspoons sugar
- ½ to 1 teaspoon ground cinnamon
- Butter-flavored cooking spray

Directions:
1. Preheat the oven to 350°F and line a shallow roasting pan with foil.
2. Pop the popcorn using your preferred method.
3. Spread the popcorn in the roasting pan and mix the sugar and cinnamon in a small bowl.
4. Lightly spray the popcorn with cooking spray and toss to coat evenly.
5. Sprinkle with cinnamon and toss again.
6. Bake for 5 minutes until just crisp then serve warm.

Nutrition Info:
- Calories 70 Total Fat 0.7g, Saturated Fat 0.1g, Total Carbs 14.7g, Net Carbs 12.2g, Protein 2.1g, Sugar 2.2g, Fiber 2.5g, Sodium 1mg

Pork Loin

Servings: 6 | Cooking Time: 20 Minutes

Ingredients:
- 1/2 lb. pork tenderloin patted dry
- Non-stick cooking spray
- 2 tbsps. garlic scape pesto
- Salt
- Pepper

Directions:
1. Adjust the temperature of the Air Fryer to 375ºF.
2. Rub all sides of the tenderloin with the non-stick cooking spray
3. Add pepper, garlic scape pesto, and salt.
4. Sprinkle the Air Fryer basket with cooking spray.
5. Place the tenderloin on the Air Fryer.
6. Cook the meal at 400°F for 10 minutes.
7. Flip over to the other side and cook for another 10 minutes on the first side.
8. Remove the food from the air fryer.
9. Serve

Nutrition Info:
- Calories: 379 kcal; Protein: 8.4g; Fat: 2.2g; Carbs: 0g

Air Fried Empanadas

Servings: 2 | Cooking Time: 20 Minutes

Ingredients:
- Square gyoza wrappers: eight pieces
- Olive oil: 1 tablespoon
- White onion: 1/4 cup, finely diced
- Mushrooms: 1/4 cup, finely diced
- Half cup lean ground beef
- Chopped garlic: 2 teaspoons
- Paprika: 1/4 teaspoon
- Ground cumin: 1/4 teaspoon
- Six green olives, diced
- Ground cinnamon: 1/8 teaspoon
- Diced tomatoes: half cup
- One egg, lightly beaten

Directions:
1. In a skillet, over a medium flame, add oil, onions, and beef and cook for 3 minutes, until beef turns brown.
2. Add mushrooms and cook for six minutes until it starts to brown. Then add paprika, cinnamon, olives, cumin, and garlic and cook for 3 minutes or more.
3. Add in the chopped tomatoes, and cook for a minute. Turn off the heat; let it cool for five minutes.
4. Lay gyoza wrappers on a flat surface add one and a half tbsp. of beef filling in each wrapper. Brush edges with water or egg, fold wrappers, pinch edges.
5. Put four empanadas in an even layer in an air fryer basket, and cook for 7 minutes at 400°F until nicely browned.
6. Serve with sauce and salad greens.

Nutrition Info:
- per serving Calories 343 |Fat 19g |Protein 18g |Carbohydrate 12.9g

Chicken In Tomato Juice

Servings: 3 | Cooking Time: 15 Minutes

Ingredients:
- 350 g chicken fillet
- 200 g tomato juice
- 100 g tomatoes
- 2 teaspoon basil
- 1 teaspoon chili
- 1 teaspoon oregano
- 1 teaspoon rosemary
- 1 teaspoon olive oil
- 1 teaspoon mint
- 1 teaspoon lemon juice

Directions:
1. Take a bowl and make the tomato sauce: combine basil, chili, oregano, rosemary, and olive oil, mint and lemon juice and stir the mixture very carefully.
2. You can use a hand mixer to mix the mass. It will make the mixture smooth.
3. Take a chicken fillet and separate it into 3 pieces.
4. Put the meat to the tomato mixture and leave for 15 minutes.
5. Meanwhile, preheat the air fryer oven to 230 C.
6. Put the meat mixture on the tray and put it in the oven for at least 15 minutes.

Nutrition Info:
- Caloric content – 258 kcal Proteins – 34.8 grams Fats – 10.5 grams Carbohydrates – 5.0 grams

Spicy Lamb Sirloin Steak

Servings: 4 | Cooking Time: 20 Minutes

Ingredients:
- 1-pound lamb sirloin steaks, pastured, boneless
- For the Marinade:
- ½ of white onion, peeled
- 1 teaspoon ground fennel
- 5 cloves of garlic, peeled
- 4 slices of ginger
- 1 teaspoon salt
- 1/2 teaspoon ground cardamom
- 1 teaspoon garam masala
- 1 teaspoon ground cinnamon
- 1 teaspoon cayenne pepper

Directions:
1. Place all the ingredients for the marinade in a food processor and then pulse until well blended.
2. Make cuts in the lamb chops by using a knife, then place them in a large bowl and add prepared marinade in it.
3. Mix well until lamb chops are coated with the marinade and let them marinate in the refrigerator for a minimum of 30 minutes.
4. Then switch on the air fryer, insert fryer basket, grease it with olive oil, then shut with its lid, set the fryer at 330 degrees F and preheat for 5 minutes.
5. Open the fryer, add lamb chops in it, close with its lid and cook for 15 minutes until nicely golden and cooked, flipping the steaks halfway through the frying.
6. When air fryer beeps, open its lid, transfer lamb steaks onto a serving plate and serve.

Nutrition Info:
- Calories: 182 CalCarbs: 3 gFat: 7 gProtein: 24 gFiber: 1 g

Asian Swordfish

Servings: 4 | Cooking Time: 6 To 11 Minutes

Ingredients:
- 4 (4-ounce) swordfish steaks
- ½ teaspoon toasted sesame oil (see Tip)
- 1 jalapeño pepper, finely minced
- 2 garlic cloves, grated
- 1 tablespoon grated fresh ginger
- ½ teaspoon Chinese five-spice powder
- ⅛ teaspoon freshly ground black pepper
- 2 tablespoons freshly squeezed lemon juice

Directions:
1. Place the swordfish steaks on a work surface and drizzle with the sesame oil.
2. In a small bowl, mix the jalapeño, garlic, ginger, five-spice powder, pepper, and lemon juice. Rub this mixture into the fish and let it stand for 10 minutes.
3. Roast the swordfish in the air fryer for 6 to 11 minutes, or until the swordfish reaches an internal temperature of at least 140°F on a meat thermometer. Serve immediately.

Nutrition Info:
- Calories: 187 Fat: 6g (29% of calories from fat) Saturated Fat: 1g Protein: 29g Carbohydrates: 2g Sodium: 132mg Fiber: 0g Sugar: 1g 3% DV vitamin A 15% DV vitamin C

Pork On A Blanket

Servings: 4 | Cooking Time: 10 Minutes

Ingredients:
- 1/2 puff defrosted pastry sheet
- 16 thick smoked sausages
- 15 ml of milk

Directions:
1. Adjust the temperature of the air fryer to 200°C and set the timer to 5 minutes.
2. Cut the puff pastry into 64 x 38 mm strips.
3. Place a cocktail sausage at the end of the puff pastry and roll around the sausage, sealing the dough with some water.
4. Brush the top of the sausages wrapped in milk and place them in the preheated air fryer.
5. Cook at 200°C for 10 minutes or until golden brown.

Nutrition Info:
- Calories: 242 kcal; Fat: 14g; Carbs: 0g; Protein: 27g

Homemade Flamingos

Servings: 4 | Cooking Time: 20 Minutes

Ingredients:
- 400g of very thin sliced pork fillets c / n
- 2 boiled and chopped eggs
- 100g chopped Serrano ham
- 1 beaten egg
- Breadcrumbs

Directions:
1. Make a roll with the pork fillets. Introduce half-cooked egg and Serrano ham. So that the roll does not lose its shape, fasten with a string or chopsticks.
2. Pass the rolls through beaten egg and then through the breadcrumbs until it forms a good layer.
3. Preheat the air fryer a few minutes at 180° C.
4. Insert the rolls in the basket and set the timer for about 8 minutes at 180o C.
5. Serve right away.

Nutrition Info:
- Calories: 482 Fat: 23.41 Carbohydrates: 0g Protein: 16.59 Sugar: 0g Cholesterol: 173gm

Nutty Chicken Nuggets

Servings: 4 | Cooking Time: 10 To 13 Minutes

Ingredients:
- 1 egg white
- 1 tablespoon freshly squeezed lemon juice
- ½ teaspoon dried basil
- ½ teaspoon ground paprika
- 1 pound low-sodium boneless skinless chicken breasts, cut into 1½-inch cubes
- ½ cup ground almonds
- 2 slices low-sodium whole-wheat bread, crumbled

Directions:
1. In a shallow bowl, beat the egg white, lemon juice, basil, and paprika with a fork until foamy.
2. Add the chicken and stir to coat.
3. On a plate, mix the almonds and bread crumbs.
4. Toss the chicken cubes in the almond and bread crumb mixture until coated.
5. Bake the nuggets in the air fryer, in two batches, for 10 to 13 minutes, or until the chicken reaches an internal temperature of 165°F on a meat thermometer. Serve immediately.

Nutrition Info:
- Calories: 249 Fat: 8g (29% of calories from fat) Saturated Fat: 1g Protein: 32g Carbohydrates: 13g Sodium: 137mg Fiber: 3g Sugar: 3g 3% DV vitamin A 2% DV vitamin C

Double Cheeseburger

Servings: 1 | Cooking Time: 18 Minutes

Ingredients:
- 2 beef patties, pastured
- 1/8 teaspoon onion powder
- 2 slices of mozzarella cheese, low fat
- 1/8 teaspoon ground black pepper
- 1/8 teaspoon salt

Directions:
1. Switch on the air fryer, insert fryer basket, grease it with olive oil, then shut with its lid, set the fryer at 370 degrees F and preheat for 5 minutes.
2. Meanwhile, season the patties well with onion powder, black pepper, and salt.
3. Open the fryer, add beef patties in it, close with its lid and cook for 12 minutes until nicely golden and cooked, flipping the patties halfway through the frying.
4. Then top the patties with a cheese slice and continue cooking for 1 minute or until cheese melts.
5. Serve straight away.

Nutrition Info:
- Calories: 670 CalCarbs: 0 gFat: 50 gProtein: 39 gFiber: 0 g

Chicken Meatballs

Servings: 6 | Cooking Time: 20 Minutes

Ingredients:
- 400 g ground chicken
- 100 g chopped dill
- 2 teaspoon olive oil
- 100 g tomato juice
- 1 teaspoon black pepper
- 1 teaspoon white pepper
- 1 egg
- 20 g milk

Directions:
1. Put the ground mix to the big mixing bowl.
2. Add chopped dill, black and white pepper and stir the mixture very carefully.
3. Add egg and stir it again.
4. Make the balls from the mixture and make the sauce from tomato juice and milk.
5. Pour the sauce into the tray and put the meatballs in it.
6. Preheat the air fryer oven to 180 C and put the meatballs in it.
7. Cook it for 20 minutes and serve immediately.

Nutrition Info:
- Caloric content – 199 kcal Proteins – 23.9 grams Fats – 8.1 grams Carbohydrates – 10.7 grams

Chocolate Chip Muffins

Servings: 6-8 | Cooking Time: 15 Minutes

Ingredients:
- 50g granulated sugar
- 125 ml of coconut milk or soymilk
- 60 ml coconut oil, liquid
- 5 ml vanilla extract
- 120g all-purpose flour
- 14g cocoa powder
- 4g baking powder
- 2g of baking soda
- A pinch of salt
- 85g chocolate chips
- 25g of pistachios, cracked (optional)
- Nonstick Spray Oil

Directions:
1. Put the sugar, coconut milk, coconut oil and vanilla extract in a small bowl, then set aside. Mix the flour, cocoa powder, baking powder, baking soda and salt in a separate bowl and set aside.
2. Mix the dry ingredients with the wet ingredients gradually, until smooth. Then join with the chocolate and pistachio.
3. Preheat the air fryer for a few minutes and set the temperature to 150°C. Grease the muffin pans with oil spray and pour the mixture until they are filled to ¾.
4. Place the muffin molds carefully in the preheated air fryer. Set the time to 15 minutes at 150°C.
5. Remove the muffins when finished cooking and let them cool for 10 minutes before serving.

Nutrition Info:
- Calories: 374 Fat: 17.31g Carbohydrates: 48.86g Protein: 9.41g Sugar: 7.73 Cholesterol: 45g

Pork Chops

Servings: 5 | Cooking Time: 15 Minutes

Ingredients:
- 4 slices of almond bread
- 5 pork chops, bone-in, pastured
- 3.5 ounces coconut flour
- 1 teaspoon salt
- 3 tablespoons parsley
- ½ teaspoon ground black pepper
- 1 tablespoon pork seasoning
- 2 tablespoons olive oil
- 1/3 cup apple juice, unsweetened
- 1 egg, pastured

Directions:
1. Switch on the air fryer, insert fryer basket, grease it with olive oil, then shut with its lid, set the fryer at 350 degrees F and preheat for 5 minutes.
2. Meanwhile, place bread slices in a food processor and pulse until mixture resembles crumbs.
3. Tip the bread crumbs in a shallow dish, add parsley, ½ teaspoon salt, ¼ teaspoon ground black pepper and stir until mixed.
4. Place flour in another shallow dish, add remaining salt and black pepper, along with pork seasoning and stir until mixed.
5. Crack the egg in a bowl, pour in apple juice and whisk until combined.
6. Working on one pork chop at a time, first coat it into the flour mixture, then dip into egg and then evenly coat with breadcrumbs mixture.
7. Open the fryer, add coated pork chops in it in a single layer, close with its lid and cook for 10 minutes until nicely golden and cooked, flipping the pork chops halfway through the frying.
8. When air fryer beeps, open its lid, transfer pork chops onto a serving plate and serve.

Nutrition Info:
- Calories: 441 CalCarbs: 28.6 gFat: 22.3 gProtein: 30.6 gFiber: 0.5 g

Tuna Wraps

Servings: 4 | Cooking Time: 4 To 7 Minutes

Ingredients:
- 1 pound fresh tuna steak, cut into 1-inch cubes
- 1 tablespoon grated fresh ginger
- 2 garlic cloves, minced
- ½ teaspoon toasted sesame oil
- 4 low-sodium whole-wheat tortillas
- ¼ cup low-fat mayonnaise
- 2 cups shredded romaine lettuce
- 1 red bell pepper, thinly sliced

Directions:
1. In a medium bowl, mix the tuna, ginger, garlic, and sesame oil. Let it stand for 10 minutes.
2. Grill the tuna in the air fryer for 4 to 7 minutes, or until done to your liking and lightly browned
3. Make wraps with the tuna, tortillas, mayonnaise, lettuce, and bell pepper. Serve immediately.

Nutrition Info:
- Calories: 288 Fat: 7g (22% of calories from fat) Saturated Fat 2g Protein: 31g Carbohydrates: 26g Sodium: 135mg Fiber: 1g Sugar: 1g 152% DV vitamin A 36% DV vitamin C

Meatloaf Slider Wraps

Servings: 6 | Cooking Time: 10 Minutes

Ingredients:
- 1-pound ground beef, grass-fed
- ½ cup almond flour
- ¼ cup coconut flour
- ½ tablespoon minced garlic
- ¼ cup chopped white onion
- 1 teaspoon Italian seasoning
- ½ teaspoon sea salt
- ½ teaspoon dried tarragon
- ½ teaspoon ground black pepper
- 1 tablespoon Worcestershire sauce
- ¼ cup ketchup
- 2 eggs, pastured, beaten

Directions:
1. Place all the ingredients in a bowl, stir well, then shape the mixture into 2-inch diameter and 1-inch thick patties and refrigerate them for 10 minutes.
2. Meanwhile, switch on the air fryer, insert fryer basket, grease it with olive oil, then shut with its lid, set the fryer at 360 degrees F and preheat for 10 minutes.
3. Open the fryer, add patties in it in a single layer, close with its lid and cook for 10 minutes until nicely golden and cooked, flipping the patties halfway through the frying.
4. When air fryer beeps, open its lid and transfer patties to a plate.
5. Wrap each patty in lettuce and serve.

Nutrition Info:
- Calories: 228 CalCarbs: 6 gFat: 16 gProtein: 13 gFiber: 2 g

Pork Fillets With Serrano Ham

Servings: 4 | Cooking Time: 20 Minutes

Ingredients:
- 400g of very thin sliced pork fillets
- 2 boiled and chopped eggs
- 100g chopped Serrano ham
- 1 beaten egg
- Breadcrumbs

Directions:
1. Make a roll with the pork fillets. Introduce half-cooked egg and Serrano ham. So that the roll does not lose its shape, fasten with a string or chopsticks.
2. Pass the rolls through the beaten egg and then through the breadcrumbs until it forms a good layer.
3. Adjust the temperature of the air fryer for a few minutes at 180° C.
4. Insert the rolls in the basket and set the timer for about 8 minutes at 180° C.
5. Serve.

Nutrition Info:
- Calories: 424 kcal; Fat: 15.15g; Carbs: 37.47g; Protein: 31.84g

Fried Pork Chops

Servings: 2 | Cooking Time: 35 Minutes

Ingredients:
- 3 cloves ground garlic
- 2 tbsps. olive oil
- 1 tbsp. of marinade
- 4 thawed pork chops

Directions:
1. In a bowl, mix the cloves of ground garlic, oil, and marinade.
2. Apply the mixture on the pork chops.
3. Put the chops in the air fryer and cook at 3600C for 35 minutes.

Nutrition Info:
- Calories: 118 kcal; Fat: 6.85g; Carbs: 0g; Protein: 13.12g

Stuffed Cabbage And Pork Loin Rolls

Servings: 4 | Cooking Time: 25 Minutes

Ingredients:
- 500g of white cabbage
- 1 onion
- 8 pork tenderloin steaks
- 2 carrots
- 4 tbsp. soy sauce
- 50g of olive oil
- Salt
- 8 sheets of rice

Directions:
1. Put the chopped cabbage in the Thermo mix glass together with the onion and the chopped carrot.
2. Select 5 seconds, speed 5. Add the extra virgin olive oil. Select 5 minutes, varoma temperature, left turn, spoon speed.
3. Cut the tenderloin steaks into thin strips. Add the meat to the Thermomix glass. Select 5 minutes, varoma temperature, left turn, spoon speed. Without beaker
4. Add the soy sauce. Select 5 minutes, varoma temperature, left turn, spoon speed. Rectify salt. Let it cold down.
5. Hydrate the rice slices. Extend and distribute the filling between them.
6. Make the rolls, folding so that the edges are completely closed. Place the rolls in the air fryer and paint with the oil.
7. Select 10 minutes, 1800C.

Nutrition Info:
- Calories: 120 Fat: 3.41g Carbohydrates: 0g Protein: 20.99g Sugar: 0g Cholesterol: 65mg

Marinated Loin Potatoes

Servings: 2 | Cooking Time: 1h

Ingredients:
- 2 medium potatoes
- 4 fillets of marinated loin
- A little extra virgin olive oil
- Salt

Directions:
1. Peel the potatoes and cut. Cut with match-sized mandolin, potatoes with a cane but very thin.
2. Wash and immerse in water 30 minutes.
3. Drain and dry well.
4. Add a little oil and stir so that the oil permeates well in all the potatoes.
5. Go to the basket of the air fryer and distribute well.
6. Cook at 1600C for 10 minutes.
7. Take out the basket, shake so that the potatoes take off. Let the potato tender. If it is not, leave 5 more minutes.
8. Place the steaks on top of the potatoes.
9. Select, 10 minutes, and 1800C for 5 minutes again.

Nutrition Info:
- Calories: 136 kcal; Fat: 5.1g; Carbs: 1.9g; Protein: 20.7g

Pork Belly

Servings: 4 | Cooking Time: 40 Minutes

Ingredients:
- 1-pound pork belly, pastured
- 6 cloves of garlic, peeled
- 1 teaspoon ground black pepper
- 1 teaspoon salt
- 2 tablespoons soy sauce
- 2 bay leaves
- 3 cups of water

Directions:
1. Cut the pork belly evenly into three pieces, place them in an instant pot, and add remaining ingredients.
2. Switch on the instant pot, then shut it with lid and cook the pork belly for 15 minutes at high pressure.
3. When done, let the pressure release naturally for 10 minutes and then do quick pressure release.
4. Rake out the pork by tongs and let it drain and dry for 10 minutes.
5. Then switch on the air fryer, insert fryer basket, grease it with olive oil, then shut with its lid, set the fryer at 400 degrees F and preheat for 5 minutes.
6. While the air fryer preheats, cut each piece of the pork into two long slices.
7. Open the fryer, add pork slices in it, close with its lid and cook for 15 minutes until nicely golden and crispy, flipping the pork halfway through the frying.
8. When air fryer beeps, open its lid, transfer pork slices onto a serving plate and serve.

Nutrition Info:
- Calories: 594 CalCarbs: 2 gFat: 60 gProtein: 11 gFiber: 0 g

Strawberry Lime Pudding

Servings: 4 | Cooking Time: 10 Minutes

Ingredients:
- 2 cups plus 2 tablespoons fat-free milk
- 2 teaspoons flavorless gelatin
- 10 large strawberries, sliced
- 1-tablespoon fresh lime zest
- 2 teaspoons vanilla extract
- Liquid stevia extract, to taste

Directions:
1. Whisk together 2 tablespoons milk and gelatin in a medium bowl until the gelatin dissolves completely.
2. Place the strawberries in a food processor with the limejuice and vanilla extract.
3. Blend until smooth then pour into a medium bowl.
4. Warm the remaining milk in a small saucepan over medium heat.
5. Stir in the lime zest and heat until steaming (do not boil).
6. Gently whisk the gelatin mixture into the hot milk then stir in the strawberry mixture.
7. Sweeten with liquid stevia to taste and chill until set. Serve cold.

Nutrition Info:
- Calories 70Total Fat 0.7g, Saturated Fat 0.1g, Total Carbs 14.7g, Net Carbs 12.2g, Protein 2.1g, Sugar 2.2g, Fiber 2.5g, Sodium 1mg

Mustard-crusted Fish Fillets

Servings: 4 | Cooking Time: 8 To 11 Minutes

Ingredients:
- 5 teaspoons low-sodium yellow mustard (see Tip)
- 1 tablespoon freshly squeezed lemon juice
- 4 (3.5-ounce) sole fillets
- ½ teaspoon dried thyme
- ½ teaspoon dried marjoram
- ⅛ teaspoon freshly ground black pepper
- 1 slice low-sodium whole-wheat bread, crumbled
- 2 teaspoons olive oil

Directions:
1. In a small bowl, stir the mustard and lemon juice. Spread this evenly over the fillets. Place them in the air fryer basket.
2. In another small bowl, mix the thyme, marjoram, pepper, bread crumbs, and olive oil. Mix until combined.
3. Gently but firmly press the spice mixture onto the top of each fish fillet.
4. Bake for 8 to 11 minutes, or until the fish reaches an internal temperature of at least 145°F on a meat thermometer and the topping is browned and crisp. Serve immediately.

Nutrition Info:
- Calories: 142 Fat: 4g (25% of calories from fat) Saturated Fat: 1g Protein: 20g Carbohydrates: 5g Sodium: 140g Fiber: 1g Sugar: 1g; 4 DV vitamin C

Mediterranean Lamb Meatballs

Servings: 4 | Cooking Time: 40 Minutes

Ingredients:
- 454g ground lamb
- 3 cloves garlic, minced
- 5g of salt
- 1g black pepper
- 2g of mint, freshly chopped
- 2g ground cumin
- 3 ml hot sauce
- 1g chili powder
- 1 scallion, chopped
- 8g parsley, finely chopped
- 15 ml of fresh lemon juice
- 2g lemon zest
- 10 ml of olive oil

Directions:
1. Mix the lamb, garlic, salt, pepper, mint, cumin, hot sauce, chili powder, chives, parsley, lemon juice and lemon zest until well combined.
2. Create balls with the lamb mixture and cool for 30 minutes.
3. Select Preheat in the air fryer and press Start/Pause.
4. Cover the meatballs with olive oil and place them in the preheated fryer.
5. Select Steak, set the time to 10 minutes and press Start/Pause.

Nutrition Info:
- Calories: 282 Fat: 23.41 Carbohydrates: 0g Protein: 16.59 Sugar: 0g Cholesterol: 73gm

Grilled Chicken

Servings: 4 | Cooking Time: 5 Minutes

Ingredients:
- 300 g chicken fillet
- 1 teaspoon mustard
- 1 teaspoon olive oil
- 1 teaspoon lemon juice
- 1 teaspoon chili
- 100 g soy sauce

Directions:
1. Slice the chicken fillet on the medium pieces.
2. Put it in the big mixing bowl and sprinkle it with soy sauce and chili.
3. Add mustard, olive oil, and lemon juice.
4. Leave the mixture for at least 10 minutes.
5. Grill it in the air fryer for 5 minutes from the both sides.
6. Serve it with fresh vegetables.

Nutrition Info:
- Caloric content – 171 kcal Proteins – 23.6 grams Fats – 7.1 grams Carbohydrates – 2.4 grams

Air Fryer Beef Empanadas

Servings: 3 | Cooking Time: 20 Minutes

Ingredients:
- 8 Goya empanada discs, defrosted
- 1 cup picadillo
- 1 egg white, blended
- 1 tsp. water
- Cooking spray

Directions:
1. Set air fryer at 325 degrees F.
2. Apply a cooking spray to the basket.
3. Place 2 tbsps. of picadillo to each disc space. Fold in half and secure using a fork. Do the same for all the dough.
4. Mix water and egg whites. Sprinkle to empanadas top.
5. Set 3 of them in your air fryer and allow to bake for minutes. Set aside and do the same for the remaining empanadas.

Nutrition Info:
- Calories:183 kcal; Carbs: 22g; Protein:11 g; Fat:5g

Steak

Servings: 2 | Cooking Time: 18 Minutes

Ingredients:
- 2 steaks, grass-fed, each about 6 ounces and ¾ inch thick
- 1 tablespoon butter, unsalted
- ¾ teaspoon ground black pepper
- 1/2 teaspoon garlic powder
- ¾ teaspoon salt
- 1 teaspoon olive oil

Directions:
1. Switch on the air fryer, insert fryer basket, grease it with olive oil, then shut with its lid, set the fryer at 400 degrees F and preheat for 5 minutes.
2. Meanwhile, coat the steaks with oil and then season with black pepper, garlic, and salt.
3. Open the fryer, add steaks in it, close with its lid and cook 10 to 18 minutes at until nicely golden and steaks are cooked to desired doneness, flipping the steaks halfway through the frying.
4. When air fryer beeps, open its lid and transfer steaks to a cutting board.
5. Take two large pieces of aluminum foil, place a steak on each piece, top steak with ½ tablespoon butter, then cover with foil and let it rest for 5 minutes.
6. Serve straight away.

Nutrition Info:
- Calories: 82 CalCarbs: 0 gFat: 5 gProtein: 8.7 gFiber: 0 g

Fish And Seafood Recipes

Fish And Seafood Recipes

Catfish With Green Beans, In Southern Style

Servings: 2 | Cooking Time: 20 Minutes

Ingredients:
- Catfish fillets: 2 pieces
- Green beans: half cup, trimmed
- Honey: 2 teaspoon
- Freshly ground black pepper and salt, to taste divided
- Crushed red pepper: half tsp.
- Flour: 1/4 cup
- One egg, lightly beaten
- Dill pickle relish: 3/4 teaspoon
- Apple cider vinegar: half tsp
- 1/3 cup whole-wheat breadcrumbs
- Mayonnaise: 2 tablespoons
- Dill
- Lemon wedges

Directions:
1. In a bowl, add green beans, spray them with cooking oil. Coat with crushed red pepper, 1/8 teaspoon of kosher salt, and half tsp. Of honey and cook in the air fryer at 400 F until soft and browned, for 12 minutes. Take out from fryer and cover with aluminum foil
2. In the meantime, coat catfish in flour. Then dip in egg to coat, then in breadcrumbs. Place fish in an air fryer basket and spray with cooking oil.
3. Cook for 8 minutes, at 400°F, until cooked through and golden brown.
4. Sprinkle with pepper and salt. In the meantime, mix vinegar, dill, relish, mayonnaise, and honey in a bowl. Serve the sauce with fish and green beans.

Nutrition Info:
- Cal 243| fat 18 g| Carbs 18 g| Protein 33 g

Crab Cake

Servings: 2 | Cooking Time: 15 Minutes

Ingredients:
- 8 ounces crab meat, wild-caught
- 2 tablespoons almond flour
- 1/4 cup red bell pepper, cored, chopped
- 2 green onion, chopped
- 1 teaspoon old bay seasoning
- 1 tablespoon Dijon mustard
- 2 tablespoons mayonnaise, reduced-fat

Directions:
1. Switch on the air fryer, insert fryer basket, grease it with olive oil, then shut with its lid, set the fryer at 370 degrees F and preheat for 5 minutes.
2. Meanwhile, place all the ingredients in a bowl, stir until well combined and then shape the mixture into four patties.
3. Open the fryer, add crab patties in it, spray oil over the patties, close with its lid and cook for 10 minutes until nicely golden and crispy, flipping the patties halfway through the frying.
4. When air fryer beeps, open its lid, transfer the crab patties onto a serving plate and serve with lemon wedges.

Nutrition Info:
- Calories: 123 CalCarbs: 5 gFat: 6 gProtein: 12 gFiber: 1 g

Frozen Shrimp With Crispy Coconut

Servings: 4 | Cooking Time: 6 Minutes

Ingredients:
- 1 Box frozen coconut shrimp
- 1 Tbsp. coconut oil

Directions:
1. Adjust the temperature of the Air Fryer to 370ºF.
2. Pour the coconut oil on the Air Fryer cooking basket.
3. Place the fish in a proper arrangement on the air fryer basket.
4. Cook for 6 minutes at 390ºF.
5. Serve.

Nutrition Info:
- Calories: 212 kcal; Fat: 14g; Protein: 11g; Carbs: 24g

Fish With Maille Dijon Originale Mustard

Servings: 1 | Cooking Time: 5 Minutes

Ingredients:
- 4 tsps. Maille Dijon Originale mustard
- 4 thick trimmed cod steaks
- 2 tbsps. Oil
- 1 tbsp. flat parsley

Directions:
1. Adjust the temperature of the Air Fryer to 350ºF.
2. Season the trimmed fish.
3. Spray Maille Dijon Originale mustard on the top side of the cod using a pastry brush.
4. Place the fish in the Air Fryer basket.
5. Cook the meal at 400ºF for 5 minutes.
6. Once cooked, you can top it with parsley.
7. Serve

Nutrition Info:
- Calories: 383 kcal; Fat: 1.8g; Carbs: 3.6g; Protein: 40.9g

Air-fried Crumbed Fish

Servings: 2 | Cooking Time: 12 Minutes

Ingredients:
- 1 mug completely dry bread crumbs.
- 1/4 mug vegetable oil.
- 4 go to pieces fillets.
- 1 beaten egg.
- 1 sliced lemon.

Directions:
1. Preheat an air fryer to 351ºF.
2. Mix bread crumbs and oil with each other in a dish. Mix up until blend comes to be loosened as well as crumbly.
3. Dip fish fillets right into the egg; shake off any type of unwanted. Dip fillets into the bread crumb mix; layer uniformly as well as completely.
4. Lay coated fillets carefully in the preheated air fryer. Prepare up until fish flakes quickly with a fork, about 12 mins. Garnish with lemon pieces.

Nutrition Info:
- Calories: 148 kcal; Carbs: 13.8g; Fat: 6.7g; Protein: 7.2g

Salmon Cakes In Air Fryer

Servings: 2 | Cooking Time: 10 Minutes

Ingredients:
- Fresh salmon fillet 8 oz.
- Egg 1
- Salt 1/8 tsp
- Garlic powder ¼ tsp
- Sliced lemon 1

Directions:
1. In the bowl, chop the salmon, add the egg & spices.
2. Form tiny cakes.
3. Let the Air fryer preheat to 390. On the bottom of the air fryer bowl lay sliced lemons—place cakes on top.
4. Cook them for seven minutes. Based on your diet preferences, eat with your chosen dip.

Nutrition Info:
- Kcal: 194, Fat: 9g, Carbs: 1g, Protein: 25g

Salmon Patties

Servings: 1 | Cooking Time: 5 Minutes

Ingredients:
- 14.75 oz. salmon.
- 1 egg.
- 1/4 mug diced onion.
- 1/2 mug bread crumbs.
- 1 tsp. dill weed.

Directions:
1. Start by cleaning the fish, eliminate the bones and also skin. Drain it.
2. Blend the egg, onion, dill weed, as well as breadcrumbs into the salmon. Mix well.
3. Shape into patties. Position them in the air fryer. Set the temperature level at 370F. For 5 minutes, after that turn them and also air fry for 5 more minutes.
4. Serve.

Nutrition Info:
- Calories: 290 kcal; Carbs: 1.2g; Protein: 27.g; Fat:18.9g

Lime-garlic Shrimp Kebabs

Servings: 2 | Cooking Time: 18 Minutes

Ingredients:
- One lime
- Raw shrimp: 1 cup
- Salt: 1/8 teaspoon
- 1 clove of garlic
- Freshly ground black pepper

Directions:
1. In water, let wooden skewers soak for 20 minutes.
2. Let the Air fryer preheat to 350F.
3. In a bowl, mix shrimp, minced garlic, lime juice, kosher salt, and pepper
4. Add shrimp on skewers.
5. Place skewers in the air fryer, and cook for 8 minutes. Turn halfway over.
6. Top with cilantro and serve with your favorite dip.

Nutrition Info:
- Calories: 76kcal | Carbohydrates: 4g | Protein: 13g |fat 9 g

Parmesan Garlic Crusted Salmon

Servings: 2 | Cooking Time: 15 Minutes

Ingredients:
- Whole wheat breadcrumbs: 1/4 cup
- 4 cups of salmon
- Butter melted: 2 tablespoons
- ¼ tsp of freshly ground black pepper
- Parmesan cheese: 1/4 cup(grated)
- Minced garlic: 2 teaspoons
- Half teaspoon of Italian seasoning

Directions:
1. Let the air fryer preheat to 400 F, spray the oil over the air fryer basket.
2. Pat dry the salmon. In a bowl, mix Parmesan cheese, Italian seasoning, and breadcrumbs. In another pan, mix melted butter with garlic and add to the breadcrumbs mix. Mix well
3. Add kosher salt and freshly ground black pepper to salmon. On top of every salmon piece, add the crust mix and press gently.
4. Let the air fryer preheat to 400 F and add salmon to it. Cook until done to your liking.
5. Serve hot with vegetable side dishes.

Nutrition Info:
- Calories 330 |Fat 19g|Carbohydrates 11g|Protein 31g

Air Fryer Salmon With Maple Soy Glaze

Servings: 4 | Cooking Time: 8 Minutes

Ingredients:
- Pure maple syrup: 3 tbsp.
- Gluten-free soy sauce: 3 tbsp.
- Sriracha hot sauce: 1 tbsp.
- One clove of minced garlic
- Salmon: 4 fillets, skinless

Directions:
1. In a ziploc bag, mix sriracha, maple syrup, garlic, and soy sauce with salmon.
2. Mix well and let it marinate for at least half an hour.
3. Let the air fryer preheat to 400F with oil spray the basket
4. Take fish out from the marinade, pat dry.
5. Put the salmon in the air fryer, cook for 7 to 8 minutes, or longer.
6. In the meantime, in a saucepan, add the marinade, let it simmer until reduced to half.
7. Add glaze over salmon and serve.

Nutrition Info:
- Calories 292| Carbohydrates: 12g| Protein: 35g|Fat: 11g|

Garlic Rosemary Grilled Prawns

Servings: 2 | Cooking Time: 10 Minutes

Ingredients:
- Melted butter: 1/2 tbsp.
- Green capsicum: slices
- Eight prawns
- Rosemary leaves
- Kosher salt& freshly ground black pepper
- 3-4 cloves of minced garlic

Directions:
1. In a bowl, mix all the ingredients and marinate the prawns in it for at least 60 minutes or more
2. Add two prawns and two slices of capsicum on each skewer.
3. Let the air fryer preheat to 180 C.
4. Cook for 5-6 minutes. Then change the temperature to 200 C and cook for another minute.
5. Serve with lemon wedges.

Nutrition Info:
- Cal 194 |Fat: 10g|Carbohydrates: 12g|protein: 26g

Lemon Pepper Shrimp In Air Fryer

Servings: 2 | Cooking Time: 10 Minutes

Ingredients:
- Raw shrimp: 1 and 1/2 cup peeled, deveined
- Olive oil: 1/2 tablespoon
- Garlic powder: ¼ tsp
- Lemon pepper: 1 tsp
- Paprika: ¼ tsp
- Juice of one lemon

Directions:
1. Let the air fryer preheat to 400 F
2. In a bowl, mix lemon pepper, olive oil, paprika, garlic powder, and lemon juice. Mix well. Add shrimps and coat well
3. Add shrimps in the air fryer, cook for 6,8 minutes and top with lemon slices and serve

Nutrition Info:
- Calories 237 |Fat 6g|Carbohydrates 11g|Protein 36g

Juicy Air Fryer Salmon

Servings: 4 | Cooking Time: 12 Minutes

Ingredients:
- Lemon pepper seasoning: 2 teaspoons
- Salmon: 4 cups
- Olive oil: one tablespoon
- Seafood seasoning: 2 teaspoons
- Half lemon's juice
- Garlic powder: 1 teaspoon
- Kosher salt to taste

Directions:
1. In a bowl, add one tbsp. of olive oil and half lemon's juice.
2. Pour this mixture over salmon and rub. Leave the skin on salmon. It will come off when cooked.
3. Rub the salmon with kosher salt and spices.
4. Put parchment paper in the air fryer basket. Put the salmon in the air fryer.
5. Cook at 360 F for ten minutes. Cook until inner salmon temperature reaches 140 F.
6. Let the salmon rest five minutes before serving.
7. Serve with salad greens and lemon wedges.

Nutrition Info:
- 132 Cal| total fat 7.4g |carbohydrates 12 g| protein 22.1g

Grilled Salmon With Lemon

Servings: 4 | Cooking Time: 20 Minutes

Ingredients:
- Olive oil: 2 tablespoons
- Two Salmon fillets
- Lemon juice
- Water: 1/3 cup
- Gluten-free light soy sauce: 1/3 cup
- Honey: 1/3 cup
- Scallion slices
- Cherry tomato
- Freshly ground black pepper, garlic powder, kosher salt to taste

Directions:
1. Season salmon with pepper and salt
2. In a bowl, mix honey, soy sauce, lemon juice, water, oil. Add salmon in this marinade and let it rest for least two hours.
3. Let the air fryer preheat at 180°C
4. Place fish in the air fryer and cook for 8 minutes.
5. Move to a dish and top with scallion slices.

Nutrition Info:
- Cal 211| fat 9g |protein 15g| carbs 4.9g

Parmesan Shrimp

Servings: 6 | Cooking Time: 10 Minutes

Ingredients:
- 2 pounds jumbo shrimp, wild-caught, peeled, deveined
- 2 tablespoons minced garlic
- 1 teaspoon onion powder
- 1 teaspoon basil
- 1 teaspoon ground black pepper
- 1/2 teaspoon dried oregano
- 2 tablespoons olive oil
- 2/3 cup grated parmesan cheese, reduced-fat
- 2 tablespoons lemon juice

Directions:
1. Switch on the air fryer, insert fryer basket, grease it with olive oil, then shut with its lid, set the fryer at 350 degrees F and preheat for 5 minutes.
2. Meanwhile, place cheese in a bowl, add remaining ingredients except for shrimps and lemon juice and stir until combined.
3. Add shrimps and then toss until well coated.
4. Open the fryer, add shrimps in it, spray oil over them, close with its lid and cook for 10 minutes until nicely golden and crispy, shaking halfway through the frying.
5. When air fryer beeps, open its lid, transfer chicken onto a serving plate, drizzle with lemon juice and serve.

Nutrition Info:
- Calories: 307 CalCarbs: 12 gFat: 16.4 gProtein: 27.6 gFiber: 3 g

Air Fryer Salmon Fillets

Servings: 2 | Cooking Time:15 Minutes

Ingredients:
- Low-fat Greek yogurt: 1/4 cup
- Two salmon fillets
- Fresh dill: 1 tbsp. (chopped)
- One lemon and lemon juice
- Garlic powder: half tsp.
- Kosher salt and pepper

Directions:
1. Cut the lemon in slices and lay at the bottom of the air fryer basket.
2. Season the salmon with kosher salt and pepper. Put salmon on top of lemons.
3. Let it cook at 330 degrees for 15 minutes.
4. In the meantime, mix garlic powder, lemon juice, salt, pepper with yogurt and dill.
5. Serve the fish with sauce.

Nutrition Info:
- Calories: 194kcal | Carbohydrates: 6g | Protein: 25g | Fat: 7g

Air Fryer Lemon Cod

Servings: 1 | Cooking Time: 10 Minutes

Ingredients:
- One cod fillet
- Dried parsley
- Kosher salt and pepper to taste
- Garlic powder
- One lemon

Directions:
1. In a bowl, mix all ingredients and coat the fish fillet with spices.
2. Slice the lemon and lay at the bottom of the air fryer basket.
3. Put spiced fish on top. Cover the fish with lemon slices.
4. Cook for ten minutes at 375F, the internal temperature of fish should be 145F.
5. Serve with microgreen salad.

Nutrition Info:
- Calories: 101kcal | Carbohydrates: 10g | Protein: 16g | Fat: 1g |

Honey & Sriracha Tossed Calamari

Servings: 2 | Cooking Time: 20 Minutes

Ingredients:
- Club soda: 1 cup
- Sriracha: 1-2 Tbsp.
- Calamari tubes: 2 cups
- Flour: 1 cup
- Pinches of salt, freshly ground black pepper, red pepper flakes, and red pepper
- Honey: 1/2 cup

Directions:
1. Cut the calamari tubes into rings. Submerge them with club soda. Let it rest for ten minutes.
2. In the meantime, in a bowl, add freshly ground black pepper, flour, red pepper, and kosher salt and mix well.
3. Drain the calamari and pat dry with a paper towel. Coat well the calamari in the flour mix and set aside.
4. Spray oil in the air fryer basket and put calamari in one single layer.
5. Cook at 375 for 11 minutes. Toss the rings twice while cooking. Meanwhile, to make sauce honey, red pepper flakes, and sriracha in a bowl, well.
6. Take calamari out from the basket, mix with sauce cook for another two minutes more. Serve with salad green.

Nutrition Info:
- Cal 252 | Fat: 38g| Carbs: 3.1g|Protein: 41g

Cilantro Lime Shrimps

Servings: 4 | Cooking Time: 21 Minutes

Ingredients:
- 1/2-pound shrimp, peeled, deveined
- 1/2 teaspoon minced garlic
- 1 tablespoon chopped cilantro
- 1/2 teaspoon paprika
- ¾ teaspoon salt
- 1/2 teaspoon ground cumin
- 2 tablespoons lemon juice

Directions:
1. Take 6 wooden skewers and let them soak in warm water for 20 minutes.
2. Meanwhile, switch on the air fryer, insert fryer basket, grease it with olive oil, then shut with its lid, set the fryer at 350 degrees F and let preheat.
3. Whisk together lemon juice, paprika, salt, cumin, and garlic in a large bowl, then add shrimps and toss until well coated.
4. Drain the skewers and then thread shrimps in them.
5. Open the fryer, add shrimps in it in a single layer, spray oil over them, close with its lid and cook for 8 minutes until nicely golden and cooked, turning the skewers halfway through the frying.
6. When air fryer beeps, open its lid, transfer shrimps onto a serving plate and keep them warm.
7. Cook remaining shrimp skewers in the same manner and serve.

Nutrition Info:
- Calories: 59 CalCarbs: 0.3 gFat: 1.5 gProtein: 11 gFiber: 0 g

Salmon With Brown Sugar Glaze

Servings: 1 | Cooking Time: 15 Minutes

Ingredients:
- 2 tbsps. Dijon mustard
- 4 (6 oz.) Boneless salmon fillets
- 1/4 Cup of packed light brown sugar
- Salt
- Ground black pepper

Directions:
1. Adjust the temperature of the Air Fryer to 3750F.
2. Sprinkle the Fryer basket with cooking spray.
3. Apply pepper and salt on the fish then place it in the Air Fryer basket.
4. In a separate small bowl, whisk together brown sugar and Dijon mustard.
5. Coat the fish properly with the mixture.
6. Cook for about 15 minutes.
7. Serve

Nutrition Info:
- Calories: 553 kcal; Fat: 9.2g; Carbs: 18.3g; Protein: 28.9g

Scallops With Creamy Tomato Sauce

Servings: 2 | Cooking Time: 10 Minutes

Ingredients:
- Sea scallops eight jumbo
- Tomato Paste: 1 tbsp.
- Chopped fresh basil one tablespoon
- 3/4 cup of low-fat Whipping Cream
- Kosher salt half teaspoon
- Ground Freshly black pepper half teaspoon
- Minced garlic 1 teaspoon
- Frozen Spinach, thawed half cup
- Oil Spray

Directions:
1. Take a seven-inch pan (heatproof) and add spinach in a single layer at the bottom
2. Rub olive oil on both sides of scallops, season with kosher salt and pepper.
3. on top of the spinach, place the seasoned scallops
4. Put the pan in the air fryer and cook for ten minutes at 350F, until scallops are cooked completely, and internal temperature reaches 135F.
5. Serve immediately.

Nutrition Info:
- Calories: 259kcal | Carbohydrates: 6g | Protein: 19g | Fat: 13g |

Crispy Fish Sticks In Air Fryer

Servings: 4 | Cooking Time: 15 Minutes

Ingredients:
- Whitefish such as cod 1 lb.
- Mayonnaise ¼ c
- Dijon mustard 2 tbsp.
- Water 2 tbsp.
- Pork rind 1&1/2 c
- Cajun seasoning ¾ tsp
- Kosher salt & pepper to taste

Directions:
1. Spray non-stick cooking spray to the air fryer rack.
2. Pat the fish dry & cut into sticks about 1 inch by 2 inches' broad
3. Stir together the mayo, mustard, and water in a tiny small dish. Mix the pork rinds & Cajun seasoning into another small container.
4. Adding kosher salt & pepper to taste (both pork rinds & seasoning can have a decent amount of kosher salt, so you can dip a finger to see how salty it is).
5. Working for one slice of fish at a time, dip to cover in the mayo mix & then tap off the excess. Dip into the mixture of pork rind, then flip to cover. Place on the rack of an air fryer.
6. Set at 400F to Air Fry & bake for 5 minutes, then turn the fish with tongs and bake for another 5 minutes. Serve.

Nutrition Info:
- Cal: 263| Fat: 16g| Net Carbs: 1g| Protein: 26.4g

Air Fryer Crab Cakes

Servings: 6 | Cooking Time: 20 Minutes

Ingredients:
- Crab meat: 4 cups
- Two eggs
- Whole wheat bread crumbs: ¼ cup
- Mayonnaise: 2 tablespoons
- Worcestershire sauce: 1 teaspoon
- Old Bay seasoning: 1 and ½ teaspoon
- Dijon mustard: 1 teaspoon
- Freshly ground black pepper to taste
- Green onion: ¼ cup, chopped

Directions:
1. In a bowl, add Dijon mustard, Old Bay, eggs, Worcestershire, and mayonnaise mix it well. Then add in the chopped green onion and mix.
2. Fold in the crab meat to mayonnaise mix. Then add breadcrumbs, not to over mix.
3. Chill the mix in the refrigerator for at least 60 minutes. Then shape into patties.
4. Let the air-fryer preheat to 350F. Cook for 10 minutes. Flip the patties halfway through.
5. Serve with lemon wedges.

Nutrition Info:
- Cal 218| Fat: 13 g| Net Carbs: 5.6 g| Protein: 16.7g

Celery Leaves And Garlic-oil Grilled

Servings: 1 | Cooking Time: 20 Minutes

Ingredients:
- 1/2 mug chopped celery leaves.
- 1 diced clove garlic.
- 2 tbsps. olive oil.
- 2 entire turbot scaled and head got rid of.
- Salt and pepper

Directions:
1. Preheat the air fryer to 390ºF.
2. Arrange the grill frying pan device in the air fryer.
3. Season the turbot with salt, pepper, garlic, as well as celery leaves.
4. Brush with oil.
5. Place on the grill pan and cook for 20 mins up until the fish ends up being flaky.

Nutrition Info:
- Calories: 269 kcal; Carbs: 3.3g; Protein: 66.2g; Fat: 25.6g

Fish Sticks

Servings: 4 | Cooking Time: 15 Minutes

Ingredients:
- 1-pound cod, wild-caught
- ½ teaspoon ground black pepper
- 3/4 teaspoon Cajun seasoning
- 1 teaspoon salt
- 1 1/2 cups pork rind
- 1/4 cup mayonnaise, reduced-fat
- 2 tablespoons water
- 2 tablespoons Dijon mustard

Directions:
1. Switch on the air fryer, insert fryer basket, grease it with olive oil, then shut with its lid, set the fryer at 400 degrees F and preheat for 5 minutes.
2. Meanwhile, place mayonnaise in a bowl and then whisk in water and mustard until blended.
3. Place pork rinds in a shallow dish, add Cajun seasoning, black pepper and salt and stir until mixed.
4. Cut the cod into 1 by 2 inches pieces, then dip into mayonnaise mixture and then coat with pork rind mixture.
5. Open the fryer, add fish sticks in it, spray with oil, close with its lid and cook for 10 minutes until nicely golden and crispy, flipping the sticks halfway through the frying.
6. When air fryer beeps, open its lid, transfer fish sticks onto a serving plate and serve.

Nutrition Info:
- Calories: 263 CalCarbs: 1 gFat: 16 gProtein: 26.4 gFiber: 0.5 g

Roasted Salmon With Fennel Salad

Servings: 4 | Cooking Time: 10 Minutes

Ingredients:
- Skinless and center-cut: 4 salmon fillets
- Lemon juice: 1 teaspoon (fresh)
- Parsley: 2 teaspoons (chopped)
- Salt: 1 teaspoon, divided
- Olive oil: 2 tablespoons
- Chopped thyme: 1 teaspoon
- Fennel heads: 4 cups (thinly sliced)
- One clove of minced garlic
- Fresh dill: 2 tablespoons, chopped
- Orange juice: 2 tablespoons (fresh)
- Greek yogurt: 2/3 cup (reduced-fat)

Directions:
1. In a bowl, add half teaspoon of salt, parsley, and thyme, mix well. Rub oil over salmon, and sprinkle with thyme mixture.
2. Put salmon fillets in the air fryer basket, cook for ten minutes at 350°F.
3. In the meantime, mix garlic, fennel, orange juice, yogurt, half tsp. of salt, dill, lemon juice in a bowl.
4. Serve with fennel salad.

Nutrition Info:
- Calories 364|Fat 30g|Protein 38g|Carbohydrate 9g

Basil-parmesan Crusted Salmon

Servings: 4 | Cooking Time: 15 Minutes

Ingredients:
- Grated Parmesan: 3 tablespoons
- Skinless four salmon fillets
- Salt: 1/4 teaspoon
- Freshly ground black pepper
- Low-fat mayonnaise: 3 tablespoons
- Basil leaves, chopped
- Half lemon

Directions:
1. Let the air fryer preheat to 400F. Spray the basket with olive oil.
2. With salt, pepper, and lemon juice, season the salmon.
3. In a bowl, mix two tablespoons of Parmesan cheese with mayonnaise and basil leaves.
4. Add this mix and more parmesan on top of salmon and cook for seven minutes or until fully cooked.
5. Serve hot.

Nutrition Info:
- Calories: 289kcal|Carbohydrates: 1.5g|Protein: 30g|Fat: 18.5g

Shrimp Scampi

Servings: 4 | Cooking Time: 12 Minutes

Ingredients:
- 1-pound shrimp, peeled, deveined
- 1 tablespoon minced garlic
- 1 tablespoon minced basil
- 1 tablespoon lemon juice
- 1 teaspoon dried chives
- 1 teaspoon dried basil
- 2 teaspoons red pepper flakes
- 4 tablespoons butter, unsalted
- 2 tablespoons chicken stock

Directions:
1. Switch on the air fryer, insert fryer pan, grease it with olive oil, then shut with its lid, set the fryer at 330 degrees F and preheat for 5 minutes.
2. Add butter in it along with red pepper and garlic and cook for 2 minutes or until the butter has melted.
3. Then add remaining ingredients in the pan, stir until mixed and continue cooking for 5 minutes until shrimps have cooked, stirring halfway through.
4. When done, remove the pan from the air fryer, stir the shrimp scampi, let it rest for 1 minute and then stir again.
5. Garnish shrimps with basil leaves and serve.

Nutrition Info:
- Calories: 221 Cal Carbs: 1 gFat: 13 gProtein: 23 gFiber: 0 g

Air Fried Cajun Salmon

Servings: 1 | Cooking Time: 20 Minutes

Ingredients:
- Fresh salmon: 1 piece
- Cajun seasoning: 2 tbsp.
- Lemon juice.

Directions:
1. Let the air fryer preheat to 180 C.
2. Pat dry the salmon fillet. Rub lemon juice and Cajun seasoning over the fish fillet.
3. Place in the air fryer, cook for 7 minutes. Serve with salad greens and lime wedges.

Nutrition Info:
- 216 Cal| total fat 19g |carbohydrates 5.6g |protein 19.2g

Salmon Cakes

Servings: 2 | Cooking Time: 12 Minutes

Ingredients:
- ½ cup almond flour
- 15 ounces cooked pink salmon
- ¼ teaspoon ground black pepper
- 2 teaspoons Dijon mustard
- 2 tablespoons chopped fresh dill
- 2 tablespoons mayonnaise, reduced-fat
- 1 egg, pastured
- 2 wedges of lemon

Directions:
1. Switch on the air fryer, insert fryer basket, grease it with olive oil, then shut with its lid, set the fryer at 400 degrees F and preheat for 5 minutes.
2. Meanwhile, place all the ingredients in a bowl, except for lemon wedges, stir until combined and then shape into four patties, each about 4-inches.
3. Open the fryer, add salmon patties in it, spray oil over them, close with its lid and cook for 12 minutes until nicely golden and crispy, flipping the patties halfway through the frying.
4. When air fryer beeps, open its lid, transfer salmon patties onto a serving plate and serve.

Nutrition Info:
- Calories: 517 CalCarbs: 15 gFat: 27 gProtein: 52 gFiber: 5 g

Other Favorite Recipes

Other Favorite Recipes

Zucchini Turkey Burgers

Servings: 5 | Cooking Time:10 Minutes

Ingredients:
- Gluten-free breadcrumbs: 1/4 cup (seasoned)
- Grated zucchini: 1 cup
- Red onion: 1 tbsp. (grated)
- Lean ground turkey: 4 cups
- One clove of minced garlic
- 1 tsp of kosher salt and fresh pepper

Directions:
1. In a bowl, add zucchini (moisture removed with a paper towel), ground turkey, garlic, salt, onion, pepper, breadcrumbs. Mix well
2. With your hands make five patties. But not too thick.
3. Let the air fryer preheat to 375 F
4. Put in an air fryer in a single layer and cook for 7 minutes or more. Until cooked through and browned.
5. Place in buns with ketchup and lettuce and enjoy.

Nutrition Info:
- Calories: 161kcal|Carbohydrates: 4.5g| Protein: 18g|Fat: 7g|

Roasted Potatoes

Servings: 4 | Cooking Time: 20 Minutes

Ingredients:
- 227g of small fresh potatoes, cleaned and halved
- 30 ml of olive oil
- 3g of salt
- 1g black pepper
- 2g garlic powder
- 1g dried thyme
- 1g dried rosemary

Directions:
1. Preheat the air fryer for a few minutes. Set it to 195°C.
2. Cover the potatoes in half with olive oil and mix the seasonings.
3. Place the potatoes in the preheated air fryer. Set the time to 20 minutes. Be sure to shake the baskets in the middle of cooking.

Nutrition Info:
- Calories: 93 Fat: 0.2g Carbohydrate: 9g Protein: 1g

Tilapia With Coconut Rice

Servings: 4 | Cooking Time: 15 Minutes

Ingredients:
- 4 (6-ounce) boneless tilapia fillets
- 1 tablespoon ground turmeric
- Salt and pepper
- 1 tablespoon olive oil
- 2 (8.8-ounce) packets precooked whole-grain rice
- 1 cup light coconut milk, shaken
- ½ cup fresh chopped cilantro
- 1 ½ tablespoons fresh lime juice

Directions:
1. Season the fish with turmeric, salt, and pepper.
2. Heat the oil in a large skillet over medium heat and add the fish.
3. Cook for 2 to 3 minutes per side until golden brown.
4. Remove the fish to a plate and cover to keep warm.
5. Reheat the skillet and add the rice, coconut milk, and a pinch of salt.
6. Simmer on high heat until thickened, about 3 to 4 minutes.
7. Stir in the cilantro and lime juice.
8. Spoon the rice onto plates and serve with the cooked fish.

Nutrition Info:
- Calories 460, Total Fat 25.2g, Saturated Fat 15.3g, Total Carbs 27.1g, Net Carbs 23.4g, Protein 34.8g, Sugar 2.4g, Fiber 3.7g, Sodium 145mg

Creamy Halibut

Servings: 6 | Cooking Time: 20 Minutes

Ingredients:
- 2 lbs. halibut fillets cut into 6 pieces
- 1 tsp. dried dill weed
- 1/2 cup light sour cream
- 1/2 cup light mayonnaise
- 4 chopped green onions

Directions:
1. Adjust the temperature of the air fryer to 390°F.
2. Season the halibut with salt and pepper.
3. Mix the onions, sour cream, mayonnaise, and dill in a bowl.
4. Spread the onion mixture evenly over the halibut fillets. Cook in the air fryer for 20 minutes. Serve warm.

Nutrition Info:
- Calories: 286 kcal; Fat: 11.3g; Carbs: 6.9g; Protein: 29.8g

Whole Wheat And Honey Pizza Dough

Servings:x | Cooking Time:x

Ingredients:
- 1 pack of active dry yeast
- 1 cup of warm water
- 2 cups of whole wheat flour
- ¼ cup of wheat germ
- 1 teaspoon of salt
- 1 tablespoon of honey

Directions:
1. Preheat your air fryer to 350 degrees F.
2. Pour some yeast in warm water and give it some 10 minutes to dissolve completely. Add the honey to the dissolved yeast.
3. Get a bigger bowl. Pour the flour, salt, and wheat germ in it.
4. Add the two mixtures together and stir thoroughly.
5. Leave it for a few minutes for the dough to rise. Roll the dough on a flour-coated pan. You may want to poke a few holes on the dough with a fork.
6. Bake the dough in your air fryer for about 5 to 10 minutes. By then, it will be crispy and tender. You can now serve it by then.

Nutrition Info:
- Calories: 83 Total Fat: 0.6g Carbohydrates: 17.4g Protein: 3.5g Sodium: 196mg

Air Fryer Tofu

Servings: 1 | Cooking Time: 5 Minutes

Ingredients:
- 16 oz block added company tofu.
- 2 tbsps. low salt soy sauce.
- 1 tbsp. additional virgin olive oil.
- 1 tsp diced garlic.
- 1/2 tsp sriracha.

Directions:
1. Press Tofu-Use a tofu press, or line a plate with paper towels. Place a block of tofu ahead as well as place more paper towels on the top of the tofu so that the tofu is sandwiched between paper towels. Place a heavy pan on top of the tofu with 4 hefty containers in addition to the pan. Enable to sit for thirty minutes.
2. When tofu is pushed piece into 1-inch dices.
3. Mix soy sauce, olive oil, garlic, as well as sriracha in a small bowl. Turn tofu halfway with marinating time to make sure all sides saturate up the sauce.
4. Set tofu in air fryer basket in a single layer. Don't jam-pack. Cook for 10 mins at 375 F. Toss at the 5-minute mark.

Nutrition Info:
- Calories:115 kcal; Fat: 4g; Carbs: 2g; Proteins: 7g

Black Bean Salad With Grilled Pork Cutlets

Servings:x | Cooking Time:x

Ingredients:
- Lime wedges for serving
- 3 thin center-cut boneless pork chops
- 2 tablespoons of orange juice
- 2 tablespoons of olive oil or canola oil
- 2 tablespoons of cider vinegar
- 2 scallions, chopped
- 1 tablespoon of lime juice
- 1 tablespoon of canola oil
- ¾ teaspoon of ground cumin
- ¾ cup of canned low-sodium black beans (should be rinsed)
- ½ cup of diced red bell pepper
- ½ cup of cooked barley
- ⅓ cup of fresh corn kernels or frozen corn niblets.
- ¼ teaspoon of salt
- ¼ teaspoon of ground pepper
- ¼ teaspoon of garlic powder
- ¼ teaspoon of dried oregano
- ¼ cup of coarsely chopped fresh cilantro (optional)
- ⅛ teaspoon of salt
- ⅛ teaspoon of ground pepper

Directions:
1. Add pepper, salt, garlic powder, 1 tablespoon of oil, and lime juice together in a bowl. Whisk them until the mixture is smooth. Dip the pork into the mixture and coat it evenly. Marinate it in the refrigerator.
2. Now, after marinating the pork, the next step is to prepare salad. Add pepper, salt, oregano, cumin, vinegar, orange juice, and oil. Whisk them together in a bowl. Set up to 2 tablespoons of dressing aside.
3. Add black beans, cilantro, scallions, corn, bell pepper, barley, and black beans to the remaining dressing after setting some aside. Toss them together. Cook the pork and discard the marinade. Cook the pork for 3 minutes before you turn it over and cook it for another 2 minutes.
4. Divide the salad between 2 plates and top each salad with a pork cutlet.

Nutrition Info:
- Calories: 48 Total Fat: 24g Cholesterol: 45mg Sodium: 431mg Potassium: 687mg Carbohydrates: 34g Dietary Fiber: 8g Protein: 24g

Chicken Cheese Fillet

Servings: 4 | Cooking Time: 15 Minutes

Ingredients:
- 2 chicken fillets
- 4 Gouda cheese slices
- 4 ham slices
- Salt and Pepper
- 1 tbsp. chopped chives

Directions:
1. Adjust the temperature of the air fryer to 180°F.
2. Cut chicken fillet into four pieces. Make a slit horizontally to the edge.
3. Open the fillet and season with salt and pepper.
4. Cover each piece with chives and cheese slice.
5. Close the fillet and wrap in a ham slice.
6. Place wrap chicken fillet into an air fryer basket and cook for 15 minutes. Serve hot.

Nutrition Info:
- Calories: 386 kcal; Total Fat: 21g; Carbs: 14.3g; Protein: 30g

Beef Fajitas

Servings: 4 | Cooking Time: 15 Minutes

Ingredients:
- 1 lbs. lean beef sirloin, sliced thin
- 1 tablespoon olive oil
- 1 medium red onion, sliced
- 1 red pepper, sliced thin
- 1 green pepper, sliced thin
- ½ teaspoon ground cumin
- ½ teaspoon chili powder
- 8 (6-inch) whole-wheat tortillas
- Fat-free sour cream

Directions:
1. Heat a large cast-iron skillet over medium heat then add the oil.
2. Add the sliced beef and cook in a single layer for 1 minute on each side.
3. Remove the beef to a bowl and cover to keep warm.
4. Reheat the skillet then add the onions and peppers – season with cumin and chili powder.
5. Stir-fry the veggies to your liking then add to the bowl with the beef.
6. Serve hot in small whole-wheat tortillas with sliced avocado and fat-free sour cream.

Nutrition Info:
- Calories 430, Total Fat 14.8g, Saturated Fat 3.2g, Total Carbs 30.5g, Net Carbs 12.9g, Protein 41.2g, Sugar 3.4g, Fiber 17.6g, Sodium 561mg

One-skillet Italian Sausage Pasta

Servings:x | Cooking Time:x

Ingredients:
- ¼ cup of grated parmesan cheese
- 8 ounces of dry penne pasta (uncooked one)
- 1 cup of tomato sauce
- 1 can of diced tomatoes with oregano, garlic, and basil (undrained one)
- 1 ¼ cups of water
- ¾ pound of Italian pork sausage

Directions:
1. The first step is to preheat your air fryer with medium heat. Then, add the sausage and cook for 5 minutes.
2. Break the sausage apart and drain it.
3. Add the pasta, tomato sauce, undrained tomatoes, and water to a skillet. Cook until it boils.
4. Now, cook it in your air fryer for about 15 minutes. By then, the pasta will be tender.
5. Bring it out and sprinkle parmesan cheese on it. You can then serve it.

Nutrition Info:
- Vitamin A: 469 IU Vitamin C: 9 mg Dietary fiber: 3 g Sugars: 5 g Saturated Fat: 4 g Protein: 15 g Sodium: 852 mg Calories: 319 kcal Iron: 2 mg Total Fat: 12 g Cholesterol: 34 mg Carbohydrate:36 mg Calcium: 89 mg

Turkey Cobb Salad

Servings: 4 | Cooking Time: None

Ingredients:
- 3 tablespoons red wine vinegar
- 3 tablespoons olive oil
- 1 tablespoon Dijon mustard
- Salt and pepper
- 8 cups fresh chopped romaine
- ¼ cup thinly sliced red onion
- 1 cup diced tomatoes
- 1 cup diced cucumber
- 4 ounces smoked turkey, sliced
- 4 slices turkey bacon, cooked and chopped
- 4 large hardboiled eggs, peeled and sliced

Directions:
1. Whisk together the vinegar, olive oil, mustard, salt, and pepper in a small bowl.
2. Divide the lettuce, red onion, tomatoes, and cucumber among four salad plates.
3. Top each with ¼ of the turkey and turkey bacon.
4. Add a sliced egg to each salad and drizzle with dressing to serve.

Nutrition Info:
- Calories 390,Total Fat 14.1gSaturated Fat 3.3g, Total Carbs 48.2g, Net Carbs 34.8g, Protein 20.3g,Sugar 3.2 Fiber 13.4g, Sodium 207mg

Almond-crusted Salmon

Servings: 4 | Cooking Time: 15 Minutes

Ingredients:
- ¼ cup almond meal
- ¼ cup whole-wheat breadcrumbs
- ¼ teaspoon ground coriander
- 1/8 teaspoon ground cumin
- 4 (6-ounce) boneless salmon fillets
- 1 tablespoon fresh lemon juice
- Salt and pepper

Directions:
1. Preheat the oven to 500°F and line a small baking dish with foil.
2. Combine the almond meal, breadcrumbs, coriander, and cumin in a small bowl.
3. Rinse the fish in cool water then pat dry and brush with lemon juice.
4. Season the fish with salt and pepper then dredge in the almond mixture on both sides.
5. Place the fish in the baking dish and bake for 15 minutes until it just flakes with a fork.

Nutrition Info:
- Calories: 232 Fat: 15g Carbohydrates: 5.89g Protein: 18.2g Sugar: 1.72g Cholesterol: 141mg

Recipe For Eight Flourless Brownies

Servings:x | Cooking Time:x

Ingredients:
- 1/8 teaspoon of salt
- 2 teaspoons of vanilla
- 1 cup of extra virgin coconut oil
- 1 cup of coconut palm sugar
- 1 cup of unsweetened cacao powder
- 4 large eggs

Directions:
1. The first thing is to preheat your oven to about 350F.
2. After that, you can mix all the ingredients listed above thoroughly. Pour the mixture into a parchment paper. Then, bake it in your air fryer for about 25 minutes or a little longer. By then, the brownie may still be soft, but it will have a little jiggle in it. Don't worry about that, just leave it for about 5 hours. It will be a little harder. Then, you can cut and eat your delicious brownies.
3. If you can't wait for up to 5 hours, you can put it in the refrigerator for about 15 minutes to an hour to speed up its cooling. It is also important to remind you that the quantities of the ingredient are for 8 brownies. You may reduce the quantities to make fewer brownies or increase them to make more, but you need to get the hang of it first before you can tweak the quantities.

Nutrition Info:
- Potassium: Negligible Calcium: Negligible Sodium: 677mg Fiber: 7g Carbohydrate: 31g Protein: 33g Saturated Fat: 3.5g Unsaturated Fat: 12g Calories: 416

Brown Rice & Lentil Salad

Servings: 4 | Cooking Time: 10 Minutes

Ingredients:
- 1-cup water
- ½ cup instant brown rice
- 2 tablespoons olive oil
- 2 tablespoons red wine vinegar
- 1-tablespoon Dijon mustard
- 1 tablespoon minced onion
- ½-teaspoon paprika
- Salt and pepper
- 1 (15-ounce) can brown lentils, rinsed and drained
- 1 medium carrot, shredded
- 2 tablespoons fresh chopped parsley

Directions:
1. Stir together the water and instant brown rice in a medium saucepan.
2. Bring to a boil then simmer for 10 minutes, covered.
3. Remove from heat and set aside while you prepare the salad.
4. Whisk together the olive oil, vinegar, Dijon mustard, onion, paprika, salt, and pepper in a medium bowl.
5. Toss in the cooked rice, lentils, carrots, and parsley.
6. Adjust seasoning to taste then stir well and serve warm.

Nutrition Info:
- Calories 1455Total Fat 4.8gSaturated Fat 0.7gTotal Carbs 8.5gNet Carbs 4.6g Protein 2.1g Sugar 1.7g Fiber 3.9g Sodium 75mg

Air Fryer Brussels Sprouts

Servings: 1 | Cooking Time: 18 Minutes

Ingredients:
- 2 cups halved brussels sprouts
- 1 tbsp. olive oil.
- 1/4 tsp. sea salt.

Directions:
1. Preheat air fryer to 375°F for 5 minutes.
2. Toss the sprouts in bowl with olive oil as well as add to the air fryer.
3. Gently spray the basket with olive oil cooking spray. Add the sprouts and also cook for 9 mins or to your desired level of crunchy.
4. Salt finished sprouts to taste.

Nutrition Info:
- Calories: 50 kcal; Carbs: 4g; Protein:1g; Fat:4g

Potato Wedges

Servings: 4 | Cooking Time: 20 Minutes

Ingredients:
- 2 large thick potatoes, rinsed and cut into wedges 102 mm long
- 23 ml of olive oil
- 3g garlic powder
- 1g onion powder
- 3g of salt
- 1g black pepper
- 5g grated Parmesan cheese
- Tomato sauce or ranch sauce, for server

Directions:
1. Cut the potatoes into 102 mm long pieces.
2. Preheat the air fryer for 5 minutes. Set it to 195°C.
3. Cover the potatoes with olive oil and mix the condiments and Parmesan cheese until they are well covered.
4. Add the potatoes to the preheated fryer. Set the time to 20 minutes.
5. Be sure to shake the baskets in the middle of cooking.
6. Serve with tomato sauce or ranch sauce.

Nutrition Info:
- Calories: 156 Fat: 8.01g Carbohydrate: 20.33g Protein: 1.98g Sugar: 0.33g Cholesterol: 0mg

Quick Fry Chicken With Cauliflower And Water Chestnuts

Servings: 2-3 | Cooking Time:x

Ingredients:
- For the quick fry
- 1½ pounds chicken thigh fillets, diced
- 1 piece, small red bell pepper, julienned
- 1 piece, thumb-sized ginger, grated
- 2 Tbsp. olive oil
- 1 clove, large garlic, minced
- 2 stalks, large leeks, minced
- 1 can, 5 oz. water chestnuts, quartered
- 1 head, small cauliflower, cut into bite-sized florets
- ¾ cups chicken stock, low sodium
- Seasonings
- 1 tsp. stevia
- 1 Tbsp. fish sauce
- ½ Tbsp. cornstarch, dissolved in
- 4 Tbsp. water
- Pinch of salt
- Pinch of black pepper, to taste
- Garnish:
- Leeks, minced
- 1 piece, large lime, cut into 6 wedges

Directions:
1. Preheat Air Fryer to 330 degrees F.
2. Pour olive oil in a pan. Swirl pan to coat. Sauté garlic, ginger, and leeks for 2 minutes. Set aside. Add in water chestnuts, cauliflower, red bell pepper, and chicken broth. Stir well. Cook for 15 minutes.
3. Meanwhile, put the chicken in the Air fryer basket. Fry until seared and golden brown.
4. Add in seasoning into the pan. Stir and cook until the juice thickens.
5. Ladle 1 portion of quick fry veggies and chicken, Garnish with leeks and lemon wedges on the side. Serve.

Nutrition Info:
- Calorie: 220Carbohydrate: 13.6g Fat: 9Protein: 30.5gFiber: 3.8g

Turkey And Zucchini Burgers With Corn On The Cob

Servings:x | Cooking Time:x

Ingredients:
- 5 ounces of ground turkey breast
- 4 1/4-inch-thick slices of pepper Jack cheese (1 oz.)
- 3 tablespoons of panko breadcrumbs
- 3 tablespoons of finely chopped red or yellow onion
- 2 whole-wheat hamburger rolls, split and toasted
- 2 teaspoons of mayonnaise
- 2 teaspoons of low-fat plain yogurt
- 2 tablespoons of finely chopped jalapeño pepper
- 1 ¼ cups of thinly sliced red cabbage
- 1 tablespoon of lime juice
- 1 tablespoon and ½ teaspoon of canola oil
- 1 ear corn, husked and halved
- ¾ teaspoon of chili powder
- ½ teaspoon of ground cumin
- ½ cup of shredded zucchini
- ¼ teaspoon of salt
- ⅛ teaspoon of ground pepper

Directions:
1. Add 1/8 teaspoon of salt, 1 tablespoon of oil, lime juice, jalapeno, and cabbage together in a bowl. In another bowl, you should combine the chili powder with the yogurt and mayonnaise.
2. Brush the corn with ½ teaspoon of oil.
3. Add 1/8 teaspoon of salt with pepper, cumin, onion, panko, zucchini, and turkey. Marsh and the items together into a paste-like mixture.
4. Cook the corn for about 7 to 10 minutes. Also, you should heat the patties until they are browned. This should take about 5 minutes of continuous heating.
5. Top the patties with cheese slices before they are done. This will allow the cheese to melt.
6. Spread the mayonnaise mixture on the cut sides of the hamburger rolls.
7. Divide the remaining slaw on the rolls. Top the burger with the roll tops and the patties before cutting the corn into half.
8. Serve half corn with a whole burger.

Nutrition Info:
- Calories: 446 Total Fat: 19g Cholesterol: 56mg Sodium: 639mg Potassium: 318mg Carbohydrates: 43g Fiber: 6g Protein: 21g

Chicken Kebabs With Pistachio Gremolata

Servings:x | Cooking Time:x

Ingredients:
- For Chicken Kebabs:
- 1/4cup of olive oil
- 1/4cup of fresh lemon juice
- 1/4teaspoon of freshly ground black pepper
- 1/2cup of Greek yogurt
- 1/2teaspoon of garlic powder
- 1/2teaspoon of onion powder
- 3pounds of boneless skinless chicken breasts or thighs, cut into 1 1/2" cubes
- 1tablespoon of honey
- 2teaspoons of sea salt
- 1teaspoon of culinary grade lavender buds
- For Pistachio Gremolata:
- 3/4cup of olive oil
- 1/4teaspoon of freshly ground black pepper to taste
- 1/2cup of Wonderful Pistachios No Shells finely chopped
- 2teaspoons of culinary grade lavender buds optional
- 1/2teaspoon of sea saltor to taste
- 1cup of flat-leaf parsley finely chopped
- Zest of 2 medium lemons finely grated
- 2garlic cloves finely minced

Directions:
1. Combine yogurt, olive oil, lemon juice, and the remaining marinade ingredients. Whisk well to combine. Pour over chicken. Toss to make chicken coated. You can refrigerate it overnight or for at least, 1 hour.
2. For gremolata, add pepper, salt, lavender, garlic, lemon zest, pistachios, and parsley together.
3. Add ½ cup of olive oil to it before you stir it very well. You should also cover and refrigerate it until when you want to serve it.
4. Air fry the kebabs for 4 minutes. Turn them over and air fry them for another 3 minutes. Reduce the heat and cook it for another 5 minutes. This will allow the chicken to be thoroughly cooked without burning on the outside.
5. Serve the chicken kebabs with some gremolata and sauce.

Nutrition Info:
- Calories: 121 Total Fat: 4g Carbohydrates: 23g Protein: 7g Sodium: 345mg

Cilantro Lime Quinoa

Servings: 6 | Cooking Time: 25 Minutes

Ingredients:
- 1 cup uncooked quinoa
- 1-tablespoon olive oil
- 1 medium yellow onion, diced
- 2 cloves minced garlic
- 1 (4-ounce) can diced green chills, drained
- 1 ½ cups fat-free chicken broth
- ¾-cup fresh chopped cilantro
- ½ cup sliced green onion
- 2 tablespoons lime juice
- Salt and pepper

Directions:
1. Rinse the quinoa thoroughly in cool water using a fine mesh sieve.
2. Heat the oil in a large saucepan over medium heat.
3. Add the onion and sauté for 2 minutes then stir in the chili and garlic.
4. Cook for 1 minute then stir in the quinoa and chicken broth.
5. Bring to a boil then reduce heat and simmer, covered, until the quinoa absorbs the liquid – about 20 to 25 minutes.
6. Remove from heat then stir in the cilantro, green onions, and limejuice.
7. Season with salt and pepper to taste and serve hot.

Nutrition Info:
- Calories 150Total Fat 4.8gSaturated Fat 0.7gTotal Carbs 8.5gNet Carbs 4.6g Protein 2.1g Sugar 1.7g Fiber 3.9g Sodium 179mg

Air-fried Asparagus

Servings: 4 | Cooking Time: 10 Minutes

Ingredients:
- 1/2 bunch asparagus, trim off the bottoms
- Olive Oil
- Salt
- Black pepper, ground

Directions:
1. In your air-fryer basket, add in the asparagus spears. Spray with the olive oil. Season with pepper and salt.
2. Set inside air-fryer and allow to bake for about 10 minutes at 400° F.
3. Serve and enjoy.

Nutrition Info:
- Calories: 118.2 kcal; Fat: 8.1g; Carbs: 10.3g; Proteins: 5.2g

Air Fried Fish And Chips

Servings:x | Cooking Time:x

Ingredients:
- Cooking spray
- 4 skinless tilapia fillets
- 2 tablespoons of water
- 2 russet potatoes, scrubbed
- 2 large eggs
- 1/2 cup of malt vinegar
- 1 cup of whole-wheat panko (Japanese-style breadcrumbs)
- 1 cup of all-purpose flour
- 1 1/4 of teaspoons kosher salt, divided

Directions:
1. You need to cut the potatoes into spirals and cook them in batches for them to come out very crispy. So, place the first batch in your air fryer basket. Spray them with cooking spray. Toss them for even coating.
2. Cook the potatoes for 10 minutes at 375 degrees F. Don't forget to turn them over after 5 minutes. After 10 minutes, they should be crispy and golden brown in color. Remove them and put them in an airtight container to keep them warm. Then you can cook the next batch.
3. When you have been able to cook them all, you can sprinkle ¼ teaspoon of salt on them.
4. Mix ½ teaspoon of salt with flour and stir them together.
5. Whisk the eggs together with some water in another bowl. Also, mix the remaining salt with panko in the third bowl.
6. Cut each of the fish fillets into 2 long strips and toss them in the flour mixture. After that, you can now dip the coated fillets in the egg mixture. Finally, dredge them in the panko mixture. Try to spray both sides of each fish fillet with cooking spray.
7. Now, it is time to cook the fish too. Place them on a single layer in your air fryer basket. Cook them at 375 degrees F for 10 minutes.
8. When they are done, you can serve the fish along with the potato spirals and 2 tablespoons of malt vinegar

Nutrition Info:
- Unsaturated Fat: 3g Sodium: 754mg Saturated Fat: 2g Protein: 44g Potassium: 24% DV Fiber: 4g Fat: 7g Carbohydrates: 46g Calories: 415 Calcium: 5% DV

Lemony Yogurt Pound Cake

Servings: x | Cooking Time: x

Ingredients:
- 1/4 teaspoon of fine salt
- 1/4 cup of low-fat milk
- 1/4 cup of extra-virgin olive oil
- 1 1/2 cups of white whole wheat flour
- 1/2 cup of plain low-fat Greek yogurt
- 1/2 teaspoon of pure vanilla extract
- Nonstick baking spray, for coating the loaf pan
- 2 teaspoons of baking powder
- Finely grated zest of 1 lemon
- 2 large egg whites
- 1 large egg

Directions:
1. Preheat your air fryer to 350 degrees F. Coat a loaf pan with baking spray.
2. Whisk the salt together with baking powder and flour. Add the yogurt to the whole eggs, egg whites, vanilla, olive oil, and milk. Whisk the mixture thoroughly until the mixture is smoothly blended.
3. Add the flour mixture to the egg mixture and stir them together.
4. Bake the new mixture in your air fryer for about 50 minutes. Insert the cake tester. If it comes out clean, it means the cake is done.
5. Allow it to cool before you divide and serve it.

Nutrition Info:
- Calories: 254 Total Fat: 8g Cholesterol: 25mg Sodium: 195mg Carbohydrates: 38g Dietary Fiber: 3g Protein: 6g

Chicken & Veggie Bowl With Brown Rice

Servings: 4 | Cooking Time: 20 Minutes

Ingredients:
- 1 cup instant brown rice
- ¼ cup tahini
- ¼ cup fresh lemon juice
- 2 cloves minced garlic
- ¼ teaspoon ground cumin
- Pinch salt
- 1 tablespoon olive oil
- 4 (4-ounce) chicken breast halves
- ½ medium yellow onion, sliced
- 1 cup green beans, trimmed
- 1 cup chopped broccoli
- 4 cups chopped kale

Directions:
1. Bring 1-cup water to boil in a small saucepan.
2. Stir in the brown rice and simmer for 5 minutes then cover and set aside.
3. Meanwhile, whisk together the tahini with ¼-cup water in a small bowl.
4. Stir in the lemon juice, garlic, and cumin with a pinch of salt and stir well.
5. Heat the oil in a large cast-iron skillet over medium heat.
6. Season the chicken with salt and pepper then add to the skillet.
7. Cook for 3 to 5 minutes on each side until cooked through then remove to a cutting board and cover loosely with foil.
8. Reheat the skillet and cook the onion for 2 minutes then stir in the broccoli and beans.
9. Sauté for 2 minutes then stir in the kale and sauté 2 minutes more.
10. Add 2 tablespoons of water then cover and steam for 2 minutes while you slice the chicken.
11. Build the bowls with brown rice, sliced chicken, and sautéed veggies.
12. Serve hot drizzled with the lemon tahini dressing.

Nutrition Info:
- Calories 435, Total Fat 20.5g, Saturated Fat 4.1g, Total Carbs 24.1g, Net Carbs 19.3g, Protein 39.9g, Sugar 1.8g, Fiber 4.8g, Sodium 196mg

Unstuffed Cabbage

Servings:x | Cooking Time:x

Ingredients:
- 1-tablespoon olive oil
- 1 small onion, chopped
- 1½ cups chopped green cabbage
- 16 precooked frozen meatballs
- 1 cup frozen cooked rice
- 2 tomatoes, chopped
- ½ teaspoon dried marjoram
- Pinch salt
- Freshly ground black pepper

Directions:
1. In a 6-inch metal bowl, combine the oil and the onion. Bake for 2 to 4 minutes or until the onion is crisp and tender.
2. Add the cabbage, meatballs, rice, tomatoes, marjoram, salt, and pepper, and stir.
3. Bake for 12 to 16 minutes, stirring once during cooking time, until the meatballs are hot, the rice is warmed, and the vegetables are tender.

Nutrition Info:
- Calories: 453; Total Fat: 20g; Saturated Fat: 7g; Cholesterol: 47mg; Sodium: 590mg;Carbohydrates: 51g; Fiber: 4g; Protein: 25g

Roasted Broccoli With Cheese Sauce

Servings:x | Cooking Time:x

Ingredients:
- 6 cups of broccoli florets (that should be about 12 oz.)
- Cooking spray
- 10 tablespoons of low-fat evaporated milk
- 1 1/2 ounce of queso fresco (fresh Mexican cheese)
- 4 teaspoons of Aji Amarillo paste
- 6 lower-sodium saltine crackers

Directions:
1. The first thing to do is to crumble the cheese. You should get about 5 tablespoons from it.
2. Spray the cooking spray on the broccoli.
3. Then, you can place the broccoli in your air fryer basket and set the temperature to 375 degrees F.
4. Cook it for about 7 to 8 minutes. By then, it will be tender-crisp.
5. Place the saltines, Aji Amarillo paste, queso fresco, and evaporated milk in a blender, and process them together until the mixture turns into a smoothie. This should not exceed 45 seconds.
6. Pour the sauce in a bowl, and microwave it on high for 30 seconds. Now, you can serve the broccoli with the cheese sauce.

Nutrition Info:
- Calories: 108 Potassium: Negligible amount Calcium: Negligible amount Fiber: 4g Sodium: 159mg Carbohydrate: 15g Protein: 8g Saturated Fat: 1g Unsaturated Fat: 1g

Italian Pork Chops

Servings: 4 | Cooking Time: 45 Minutes

Ingredients:
- 4 pork chops, boneless
- 3 garlic cloves, minced
- 1 tsp. dried rosemary, crushed
- ¼ tsp. pepper
- ¼ tsp. sea salt

Directions:
1. Preheat the oven to 425 F/ 218 C.
2. Line baking tray with cooking spray and season pork chops with pepper and salt.
3. Combine garlic and rosemary and rub all over pork chops.
4. Place pork chops in a prepared baking tray.
5. Roast pork chops in preheated oven for 10 minutes.
6. Turn oven temperature to 350 F/ 180 C and roast for 25 minutes.
7. Serve and enjoy

Nutrition Info:
- Calories 261Fat 19.9 g, Carbohydrates 1 g,Sugar 0 g,Protein 18.1 g, Cholesterol 69 mg

Macaroni And Cheese Recipe

Servings:x | Cooking Time:x

Ingredients:
- 2 cups of shredded cheddar cheese
- 2 cups of milk
- A pinch of ground black pepper
- ½ teaspoon of salt
- ¼ cup of all-purpose flour
- ¼ cup of butter
- A box of elbow macaroni

Directions:
1. Add a pinch of salt to a large pot of water and boil it.
2. Cook the macaroni with water in your air fryer. Continue cooking it until it is done and firm to bite. This should not take more than 8 minutes. You can then drain it off.
3. Melt the butter with medium heat and mix it with flour. Add pepper and salt to the mixture and stir thoroughly. This will take only 5 minutes. Pour the milk in the mixture and continue to stir it. This should take another 5 minutes. You can then add some cheddar cheese to the mixture. You need to continue to stir it until the cheese is melted. This will take another 3 to 5 minutes. Gently fold the macaroni into the cheese sauce (the mixture), and it is ready. You can serve it.

Nutrition Info:
- Calories: 238 Fiber: 1g Calcium: Negligible amount Potassium: Negligible amount Saturated Fat: 2g Unsaturated Fat: 1g Protein: 5g Carbohydrate: 46g

Mashed Butternut Squash

Servings: 6 | Cooking Time: 25 Minutes

Ingredients:
- 3 pounds whole butternut squash (about 2 medium)
- 2 tablespoons olive oil
- Salt and pepper

Directions:
1. Preheat the oven to 400°F and line a baking sheet with parchment.
2. Cut the squash in half and remove the seeds.
3. Cut the squash into cubes and toss with oil then spread on the baking sheet.
4. Roast for 25 minutes until tender then place in a food processor.
5. Blend smooth then season with salt and pepper to taste.

Nutrition Info:
- Calories 90Total Fat 4.8gSaturated Fat 0.7gTotal Carbs 8.5gNet Carbs 4.6g Protein 2.1g Sugar 1.7g Fiber 3.9g Sodium 4mg

Air Fried Artichoke Hearts

Servings: 2-3 | Cooking Time:x

Ingredients:
- 1 pound frozen artichoke hearts, thawed, quartered
- 1-cup plain yogurt, low fat
- 2 eggs, whisked
- 1 cup almond flour, finely milled
- 1 cup almond flour, coarsely milled
- 1 small lime, sliced into wedges, pips removed
- ½ cup sour cream, reduced fat
- Pinch of sea salt

Directions:
1. Preheat Air Fryer to 330 degrees F.
2. In a bowl, combine yogurt and salt. Soak artichoke hearts for at 15 minutes. Drain. Discard yogurt.
3. Dredge artichokes in almond flour first, then into eggs, and into coarse-milled almond flour.
4. Layer artichoke hearts into the Air Fryer basket. Fry for 5 minutes or until golden brown on all sides. Drain on paper towels. Squeeze limejuice. Serve with lime wedges and sour cream on the side.

Nutrition Info:
- Calorie: 67Carbohydrate: 7g Fat: 3g Protein: 2g Fiber: 1g

28 Day Meal Plan

	Breakfast	Lunch	Dinner
Day 1	Cornbread	Lemon Pepper Chicken Breast	Tuna Wraps
Day 2	Muffins Sandwich	Meatloaf Slider Wraps	Double Cheeseburger
Day 3	Tofu Scramble	Buttermilk Chicken In Air-fryer	Chocolate Chip Muffins
Day 4	Blueberry Buns	Pork Chops	Zucchini Turkey Burgers
Day 5	Breakfast Cheese Bread Cups	Breaded Chicken With Seed Chips	Roasted Potatoes
Day 6	Garlic Bread	Chicken Meatballs	Tilapia With Coconut Rice
Day 7	Breakfast Muffins	Crispy Chicken Thighs	Creamy Halibut
Day 8	Breakfast Pizza	Nutty Chicken Nuggets	Whole Wheat And Honey Pizza Dough
Day 9	Cinnamon And Cheese Pancake	Jerk Style Chicken Wings	Air Fryer Tofu
Day 10	Blueberry Muffins	Homemade Flamingos	Chicken Cheese Fillet
Day 11	Sweet Nuts Butter	Air Fried Blackened Chicken Breast	Beef Fajitas
Day 12	Cauliflower Potato Mash	Pork On A Blanket	One-skillet Italian Sausage Pasta
Day 13	Cauliflower Hash Browns	Crispy Ranch Air Fryer Nuggets	Turkey Cobb Salad
Day 14	Fried Egg	Asian Swordfish	Almond-crusted Salmon

	Breakfast	Lunch	Dinner
Day 15	Baked Eggs	Orange Chicken Wings	Recipe For Eight Flourless Brownies
Day 16	Tortilla	Spicy Lamb Sirloin Steak	Air Fryer Brussels Sprouts
Day 17	Santa Fe Style Pizza	Southwest Chicken In Air Fryer	Brown Rice & Lentil Salad
Day 18	Pancakes	Chicken In Tomato Juice	Potato Wedges
Day 19	Zucchini And Walnut Cake With Maple Flavor Icing	Air Fried Maple Chicken Thighs	Cilantro Lime Quinoa
Day 20	Air Fryer Scrambled Egg	Air Fried Empanadas	Air-fried Asparagus
Day 21	Scotch Eggs	Chicken Wings	Air Fried Fish And Chips
Day 22	French Toast In Sticks	Pork Loin	Lemony Yogurt Pound Cake
Day 23	Cocotte Eggs	Buttermilk Fried Chicken	Chicken & Veggie Bowl With Brown Rice
Day 24	Morning Mini Cheeseburger Sliders	Cinnamon Spiced Popcorn	Unstuffed Cabbage
Day 25	Air Fried Sausage	Air Fryer Chicken Cheese Quesadilla	Fish And Vegetable Tacos
Day 26	Avocado Taco Fry	Short Ribs	Chicken Sandwich
Day 27	Zucchini Bread	Garlic-roasted Chicken With Creamer Potatoes	Warm Chicken And Spinach Salad
Day 28	Peanut Butter & Banana Breakfast Sandwich	Herbed Lamb Chops	Mushroom Oatmeal

Appendix : Recipes Index

A

Air Fried Artichoke Hearts   94
Air Fried Blackened Chicken Breast   39
Air Fried Cajun Salmon   78
Air Fried Cheesy Chicken Omelet   30
Air Fried Empanadas   54
Air Fried Fish And Chips   90
Air Fried Maple Chicken Thighs   41
Air Fried Sausage   20
Air Fryer Avocado Fries   25
Air Fryer Beef Empanadas   64
Air Fryer Brussels Sprouts   87
Air Fryer Buffalo Cauliflower   30
Air Fryer Chicken Cheese Quesadilla   43
Air Fryer Crab Cakes   75
Air Fryer Crisp Egg Cups   25
Air Fryer Egg Rolls   32
Air Fryer Lemon Cod   72
Air Fryer Pork Chop & Broccoli   44
Air Fryer Roasted Corn   31
Air Fryer Salmon Fillets   71
Air Fryer Salmon With Maple Soy Glaze   69
Air Fryer Scrambled Egg   18
Air Fryer Tofu   82
Air-fried Asparagus   90
Air-fried Crumbed Fish   67
Almond-crusted Salmon   85
Asian Swordfish   56
Avocado Egg Rolls   30
Avocado Taco Fry   21

B

Baked Eggs   16
Balsamic Cabbage   27
Basil-parmesan Crusted Salmon   77
Beef Fajitas   84
Black Bean Salad With Grilled Pork Cutlets   83
Blueberry Buns   12
Blueberry Muffins   14
Breaded Chicken Tenderloins   47

Breaded Chicken With Seed Chips   38
Breakfast Cheese Bread Cups   13
Breakfast Muffins   13
Breakfast Pizza   14
Broccoli Mash   22
Brown Rice & Lentil Salad   86
Bruschetta   22
Brussels Sprouts   32
Buffalo Chicken Hot Wings   46
Buttermilk Chicken In Air-fryer   37
Buttermilk Fried Chicken   42

C

Catfish With Green Beans, In Southern Style   66
Cauliflower Hash Browns   15
Cauliflower Potato Mash   15
Celery Leaves And Garlic-oil Grilled   75
Charred Bell Peppers   25
Cheesy Bell Pepper Eggs   28
Cherry Pies   33
Chicken & Veggie Bowl With Brown Rice   91
Chicken Cheese Fillet   83
Chicken Cheesey Quesadilla In Air Fryer   43
Chicken In Tomato Juice   55
Chicken Kebabs With Pistachio Gremolata   89
Chicken Meatballs   58
Chicken Sandwich   49
Chicken Skewers With Yogurt   48
Chicken Wings   41
Chocolate Chip Muffins   58
Cilantro Lime Quinoa   89
Cilantro Lime Shrimps   73
Cinnamon And Cheese Pancake   14
Cinnamon Spiced Popcorn   53
Cocotte Eggs   20
Cornbread   11
Crab Cake   66
Creamy Fennel   28
Creamy Halibut   81
Crispy Air Fryer Brussels Sprouts   35
Crispy Chicken Thighs   38
Crispy Fish Sticks In Air Fryer   74
Crispy Ranch Air Fryer Nuggets   39

D

Double Cheeseburger   57

F

Fish And Vegetable Tacos   52
Fish Club Sandwich   34
Fish Sticks   76
Fish With Maille Dijon Originale Mustard   67
French Toast In Sticks   19
Fried Egg   16
Fried Garlic Green Tomatoes   29
Fried Lemon Chicken   44
Fried Pork Chops   61
Frozen Shrimp With Crispy Coconut   67

G

Garlic & Cheese Potatoes   24
Garlic Bread   13
Garlic Parmesan Chicken Tenders   47
Garlic Rosemary Grilled Prawns   69
Garlic-roasted Chicken With Creamer Potatoes   43
Green Beans   28
Grilled Chicken   64
Grilled Salmon With Lemon   70

H

Ham And Cheese Stuffed Chicken Burgers   45
Herbed Lamb Chops   52
Herbed Radish Sauté   35
Homemade Flamingos   56
Honey & Sriracha Tossed Calamari   72
Honey Chili Chicken   26

I

Italian Pork Chops   93

J

Jamaican Jerk Pork In Air Fryer   49
Jerk Style Chicken Wings   38
Juicy Air Fryer Salmon   70

K

Kale And Walnuts   34

L

Lemon Chicken With Basil   45
Lemon Pepper Chicken Breast   37
Lemon Pepper Shrimp In Air Fryer   70
Lemon Rosemary Chicken   46
Lemony Yogurt Pound Cake   91
Lime-garlic Shrimp Kebabs   68

M

Macaroni And Cheese Recipe   93
Marinated Loin Potatoes   61
Mashed Butternut Squash   94
Meatloaf Slider Wraps   60
Mediterranean Lamb Meatballs   63
Mini Popovers   27
Morning Mini Cheeseburger Sliders   20
Muffins Sandwich   11
Mushroom Oatmeal   42
Mustard-crusted Fish Fillets   63

N

Nutella Smores   29
Nutty Chicken Nuggets   57

O

One-skillet Italian Sausage Pasta   84
Onion Rings   31
Orange Chicken Wings   40

P

Pancakes　17
Parmesan Garlic Crusted Salmon　69
Parmesan Shrimp　71
Peanut Butter & Banana Breakfast Sandwich　22
Popcorn Chicken In Air Fryer　50
Pork Belly　62
Pork Chops　59
Pork Fillets With Serrano Ham　60
Pork Loin　54
Pork On A Blanket　56
Pork Rind Nachos　47
Potato Wedges　87

Q

Quick Fry Chicken With Cauliflower And Water Chestnuts　88

R

Recipe For Eight Flourless Brownies　86
Roasted Broccoli With Cheese Sauce　92
Roasted Peanut Butter Squash　32
Roasted Potatoes　80
Roasted Salmon With Fennel Salad　76

S

Salmon Cakes In Air Fryer　68
Salmon Cakes　78
Salmon Fries　27
Salmon Patties　68
Salmon With Brown Sugar Glaze　73
Santa Fe Style Pizza　17
Scallops With Creamy Tomato Sauce　74
Scotch Eggs　19
Short Ribs　53
Shrimp Scampi　77
Southwest Chicken In Air Fryer　40
Spicy Lamb Sirloin Steak　55
Spinach And Artichokes Sauté　29
Steak　64
Strawberry Lime Pudding　62
Stuffed Cabbage And Pork Loin Rolls　61
Sweet Nuts Butter　15

T

Tasty Chicken Tenders 48
Tilapia With Coconut Rice 81
Tofu Scramble 12
Tortilla 16
Tuna Wraps 59
Turkey And Zucchini Burgers With Corn On The Cob 88
Turkey Cobb Salad 85

U

Unstuffed Cabbage 92

V

Vegetable Spring Rolls 24

W

Warm Chicken And Spinach Salad 53
Whole Wheat And Honey Pizza Dough 82

Z

Zucchini And Walnut Cake With Maple Flavor Icing 18
Zucchini Bread 21
Zucchini Fritters 26
Zucchini Gratin 33
Zucchini Turkey Burgers 80

Printed in Great Britain
by Amazon

36236705R00059